Rantings
of an
American Madman

By Wayne Beemer (Big W)

Contents

Preface

I am truly in despair. This Country has completely moved in a direction which I can not abide by or understand.

Racism has reared it's ugly head back up! Poor Dr. Martin Luther King is spinning in his grave. What with the Supreme Court of the United States striking down Article 4 of the Voting Rights Act, Southern States pushing an agenda of voter suppression, incarceration rates of minorities ever-increasing, anti-immigration, and the Kangaroo Courts making a mockery of the law.

Christian Extremism permeating the land like a plague of locusts. Anti abortion legislation pushed and passed in just about every Red State, 1000 plus Bills to restrict abortion and contraception, including at the Federal level.

Woman's health being systematically taken away from them in Biblical fashion. Tell me where is sanity? The inmates have truly taken over the asylum.

Corporations have usurped the people in power and speech, they literally hold the ear and the pocket of the politicians. The poor and downtrodden are spit on, and the super wealthy are put up on a pedestal. Corporations get all the breaks and the people get nothing.

America is in decline and at an alarming rate. Half the people are brainwashed by ideology and another third just don't care at all as they are mesmerized by the shiny objects. Or they are too busy working their fingers to the bone just trying to keep up with the bills.

Planned obsolescence and consumerism is engrained and rampant. We are destroying and squandering our natural resources so fast there soon will be nothing left to exploit. Profit's go only to the rich, sacrifice only to the middle classes and the poor. Privatized profit's and Socialized risk. Everything is a scam, a con, a flim-flam. Nothing is real, it's all just an illusion designed to suck the life and money out of us. Maybe Timothy Leary was right...

The musings on the following pages represent articles I have written, things I have posted out on Facebook, counter arguments for various right wing talking points, and things I wrote just because I was so angry I needed to vent somewhere.

About the Author

Hi my name is Wayne Beemer and I was born in Manhattan, raised in Queens, and lived on Long Island for many years. That is where my wife Heather and I raised our two daughters, Rose and Melanie. In 2003, after the 9/11 attacks drove housing prices up on Long Island, it was advantageous for us to sell our home there and move out to Ohio closer to where some of my wife's family is. My daughter Melanie decided to stay in New York where she finished her degree in Chemistry and still lives with a family of her own now after the birth of my grandson Matteo in 2011. Rose moved out to Ohio with us initially, but has moved around a bit as she expanded on her career in Healthcare Administration and finished her MBA.

I have a Technical Certificate degree in Machine Building and have worked in store fixtures and architectural woodwork as a purchasing agent as well as a Director. I also was a Director of an aerospace instrumentation engineering company called Computer Instruments Corp. More Recently I was a subcontract manager and negotiator for Executive Jet Management, a NetJets Company. Somewhere in between I was a bar and grill owner as well.

I Currently teach and moderate on a public

website called stockhideout.com I teach Micro and Macro Economics, Finance, Fundamental and Technical analysis as it relates to investing and stock trading.

I have had licenses in Real Estate, and as a Certified Financial adviser. I tutor OSU students and others in Math, English, Science, and Economics.

I write freelance under a pseudonym and have had articles published on major news websites.

I am an avid history buff and a news junkie. I read more before breakfast than most people read in a Month.

I consider myself a "Recovering" Republican. When I lived in NY and for most of my adult life I was a registered Republican. I was a Liberal Republican and stand with "Trust Busting", "Progressivism", conservation of public land and parks and the "Square Deal" of Teddy Roosevelt. The equal rights of all people and progressive expansion of Abe Lincoln. The progress and expansion of highways, seaways, and commerce of Dwight Eisenhower.

Currently I consider myself as Independent and "caucus" with the local Democrats. After the disaster that was George W Bush, I had to leave the GOP as their Extremism and Religious Right agenda no longer squares with my political beliefs.

I am an active member of the 99% of Newark and Licking County Ohio an affiliate of movetoamend.org

Like our founding Fathers I am a Christian Deist and Constitutionalist.

I stand with the underdog, and the people's Rights above politics, Government, Corporation, or Party. I am very Pro Choice, Pro Marriage Equality, Pro Gun Control, though I do believe in the Second Amendment and do own firearms.

I am pretty much against whatever Republicans and the Tea Party is for.

I am for an alternative, sustainable, and renewable energy economy, I am an economic Keynesian, Pro Recycling, Anti Pollution, I know for sure that Climate Change is happening, Pro Immigration, Pro Dream Act, Pro ERA, for prison reform, for strongly regulating banks, and I want a strong EPA. I want clean air and water. I am Pro Diplomacy and Anti War.

I believe we should look at other countries who have solved problems and just do what they do. I believe in Socialized Healthcare and Investing in Public Education.

This book started out life as a number of posts to social media in response to Conservative, Libertarian, Republican, and Tea party friends and family who would post the most outrageous things. Blatant lies and hypocrisy that just had to be answered with truth, facts and reason. After a while I had so many saved from these online debates I had an idea to put them in an outline and create a book to help other Progressives and Liberals debate their friends and family. This is my first attempt at an actual book, I hope it helps...

Acknowledgment and Introduction

I want to explain what this book is. It is a collage of random thoughts and ideas I put together by looking things up online to respond to social media posts and news organization posts. Quite frankly I went to so many websites and sources that there is no way of looking them all up and giving credit to all of those sites that I poached information from. The one thread of all of them is that I tried to use legitimate sites like census.gov, whitehouse.gov, bls.gov, gao.gov, etc... I believe that I researched each talking point enough that the responses I wrote are truthful and reasonably accurate, I did round numbers, and in some instances used the higher number of a range. But still in all I believe I can defend my posts with some confidence.

Typically I would copy and paste tid-bit's and then proceed to modify the contents. On occasion, I would use the whole article and add some additional thoughts. I will attempt to acknowledge as many as I can remember here. Keeping in mind that the idea was to use this information to debate online. Subsequently I wrote so much that I posted them all together into an outline so as to make the random thoughts fit within a structure. As you read through this understand that most of the time it was thrown together in anger quickly to fire back at some loathsome troll at the other end of somewhere. While I have tried to refine and polish the pieces, this is my first attempt at any writing of this magnitude, and please forgive me if I borrowed some of your words. Below is a list of sources.

"8 reasons why Ronald Reagan was the worst president of our lifetime"
By Robert Sobel

"The 14 Characteristics of Fascism" by Dr. Lawrence Britt

"The 7 Types Of Republicans And How To Debate Them"
By Matthew Desmond

Our Pledge of Allegiance and the Myth of "One Nation Under God"
By Allen Clifton

What A Nation Might Look Like Built on Republican Ideology
By Allen Clifton

The Republican De-Evolution from Political Party to Domestic Terrorists
by Allen Clifton

I wish to acknowledge the following online sources of inspiration; 27east, aacn.nche.edu, aattp, abc, abortion.procon, administrativelaw, ag.arizona.edu, agasm, aljazeera, all, alternet, amazon, americablog, americanbar, americanmagazine, anchorrising, aol, apwu, archive, atheism.about, atlasshrugs2000, aw.upenn, ayea, baldwin-white, baltimoresun, bbc, beforeitnews, betsypage, bhamfree, bidstrup, biglizards, billiadsdigest, billmoyers, blog.heritage, blogs.ajc, bls.gov, Blu-thoth, bluemassgroup, boards.straightdope, bostonmagazine, boundless, business.time, businessinsider, buzzfeed, caliber.ca.gov, catholic-convert, cbsnews, cec7, census.gov, chronicle, citizenwarrior, cnn, codepinkforpeace, coffmanhouse.gov, conversationaltheology, crankyflier, crecentok, criminalizeconservatism, dailykos, dallasnews, debate, debate, debatecoache, defendingthetruth, democraticunderground, denverpost, dnipogo, docstoc, dol.gov, downsizinggovernment, downtrend, drugwarrent, dwardmac, economist, ejas.revues, endoftheamericandream, english.stackechange, epi, everything2, examiner, facebook, fairaccess, faithfacts, fallibleblogma, fdic, forbes, forwardprogressives, freakoutnation, fredrickleatherman, freedomshrine, freerepublic, fromthewilderness, frontpagemag, fs.usa.gov, gao.gov, ghanabusines, globalreaserch, godfatherpolitics, goodreads, gov.uk, granitegrok, greatlakes-seaway, groobiecat, gunsandammo, hereandnow, higered.mcgraw-hill, historicpages, hotair, hubpages, huffingtonpost, humanevents,

humpdayreport, ign, imdb, imf, indeed,
inperspective, intelligentdiscontent, isrevie,
jaylip.fatcow, jezabel, joeabo, jonathanturley,
keepamericaatwork, keimena11, kevinmd,
knoxviews, kpic, kunstler, law.du, learnvest,
legalinsurrection, lifesitenews, littleblackblog,
lowellsun, lubbockonline, mardel, marklynas,
matttaibbi, mcimaps, mediaed, mediapolitic,
metabunk, michaelshermer, mikechurch,
mixedracestudies, monorealism, morganstanley,
mosulfamily, msn, msnbc, mtholyoke,
nationalskillscoalition, nationofchange, ncsl,
negotiationlawblog, netsidebar,
newlyweds.about, neworldeview, newrepublic,
news, newscorpse, newsminer,
newsobserveronline, northfloridaindians,
nps.gov, nullapoena, nyls, nytelecom, nyu.edu,
oceana, oig.dot.gov, onpoint.bur, ontheissues,
patheos, pathos, paulkrugman, pbs, pc.gov,
pewresearch, pilgrimpathways, politico,
politicsoffootball.wordpress, prezi, princton.edu,
propublica, propublica, pushingthesky, quizlet,
readthehook, realclearpolitics, rebelcapitalist,
reddit, redrawca, redrawingthelines, redstate,
republicannutclub, reuters, rhrealitycheck,
riverbendblog, robertreich, rollingstone,
rushlimbaugh, salon, saov.tr,
scholarship.shu.edu, scientificamerican, scribd,
seriousgivers, sharepoint.gru.wvu.edu,
shieldmutual, shmoop, showbams, snopes,
sodahead, southernstudies, spokeo, starbucks,

stlouisfed, streetlaw, sulia, swankivy, tdnews, teatime-mag, theapcl, theblueplanet, theburningplatform, thechristainleftblog, thechristiansciencemonitor, thedailybanter, thedailybeast, theguardian, thehighlandsun, thehill, thejanedough, themattwalshblog, themiamihearald, themonkeycage, thenewalexandrialibery, thenotebook, thenytimes, theodorerooseveltcenter, theplainsatisfactions, therealmcteag, thesimpledollar, thesleazebagreport, thesleazereport, thetradingreport, thetruthaboutcars, thewashingtontimes, thinkprogress, timothymccandles.wordpress, topdocumentaryfilms, topix, townhall, transcripts.cnn, turnncblue, tuscancitizen, Uglyhedgehog, unitedforthepeople, usainsurancenet, usapolitics, utexas.edu, utm.edu, vox-nova, wagingpeace, washingtonmonthly, washingtonpost, washingtonsblog, wealink, webmd, wfaa, whatreallyhappened, whisleblower, whitehouse.gov, wikipedia, wildernesswithin, wired, wisegeek, wnd, wpusa, yahoo, yelp, zerohedge, zfacts, and hundreds more I am sure that I have visited and read... while I did actually plagiarize check all content, I am sure similar wording is present. Hopefully I have recognized you as having provided content and ideology.

I am dedicating this, my first actual book to my dear friend Paul Prizzia, A good Man and Father. Paul is an outstanding citizen, a good practicing Catholic, and a steadfast Conservative. While Paul and I almost never agree on political issues, he has been an inspiration and motivator to me when needed, a friend through good times and bad. Been on the receiving end of way too many of my rants and posts. I love you like a Brother and wish to thank you for being there for me these many years.

Old School Republicans

Fact, Today's GOP does not represent even a fraction of what it used to. We have heard it said over and over. "This is not your Father's Republican party."

Republicans of the last generation were pro union, pro Labor and raised the minimum wage. Their platform included expanding Social Security, shoring up workman's compensation, increasing pension benefit's, and believe it or not, wage increases. They called for changes to the anti union Taft-Hartley Act to "More effectively protect the rights of labor unions" and to "assure equal pay for equal work regardless of sex."

Additional and better education, training of doctors and scientists, and had a history of supporting "Enlarged Federal assistance for construction of hospitals, emphasizing low-cost care of chronic diseases and the special problems of older persons, and increased Federal aid for medical care of the needy."

The Republican platform supported "self-government, national suffrage and representation in the Congress of the United States for residents of the District of Columbia." With regards to ending discrimination against racial minorities, the party took pride that "more progress has been made in this field under the present Republican Administration than in any similar period in the last 80 years." It also recommended to Congress "the submission of a constitutional amendment providing equal rights for men and women." it's section on immigration actually recommended expanding immigration to America, supporting "the extension of the Refugee Relief Act of 1953 in resolving this difficult refugee problem which resulted from world conflict."

Can you imagine that? A Republican party that was for Unions, workers, the elderly, Immigration, and genuine reform? Where exactly did all of those Republicans go? During the 1950s the GOP had no issue with a top tax rate of 92%, that's correct 92% unfathomable by Today's standards, yet we had full employment, a robust GDP, and virtually no deficit. These are the Good Old Days we hear so much about and what they want to take their County back to? 92% Tax rates, oh no, I don't think so...

Abe Lincoln

The Republican Party, also commonly called the GOP, for "Grand Old Party," is one of the two major political parties in the United States. The second being the Democratic Party.

Founded by anti-slavery activists in 1854, Republicans dominated politics nationally for most of the period from 1860 to 1932. There have been 18 Republican presidents, the first was Abraham Lincoln. Hence the term "Party of Lincoln"

Republicans were originally a group of anti-slavery activists, modernizers, ex-Whigs, and ex-Free Soilers, Whigs and Free Soilers were defunct political parties. The GOPs principal rivals was the Democrats who's base was mainly in the South.

Their primary issue was slavery, their slogan was "Free Labor, Free Land, Free Men," "Free labor" referred to GOP opposition to slave labor and belief in the cause of independent craftsmen and businessmen. "Free land" referred to their opposition to the plantation type system where slave owners would buy up all the good farm land, leaving all of the the independent farmers the leftover lesser valued properties.

The GOP supported business, the gold standard, high tariffs to promote economic growth, high wages and high profit's, generous pensions for Union veterans, and the annexation of Hawaii. They also supported Protestants who wanted Prohibition. As the northern states economy boomed with industry, railroads, mines, fast-growing cities and prosperous agriculture, the Republicans took credit and promoted policies to keep that growth going.

It is of great note to understand that Lincoln was considered a Liberal, and freeing the slaves a liberal issue.

Theodore (Teddy) Roosevelt

Theodore "TR" Roosevelt, Jr. our 26th President was a Progressive and what I would call a True Conservative. Roosevelt was widely known as a naturalist, explorer, hunter, author, and soldier. He was just as famous for those things as for being a politician. Roosevelt the title of youngest President up till then, he was 42 years old when sworn in.

Roosevelt dealt with striking mine workers thru a commission he set up which gave the miners higher pay and less working hours.

Roosevelt signed The Meat Inspection Act of 1906 along with The Pure Food and Drug Act. The Meat Inspection Act made labels clear and easy to understand. omitted preservatives that contained harmful chemicals. The Pure Food and Drug Act stopped impure products from being made or falsely labeled, sold, or shipped. Roosevelt was also involved with the American School Hygiene Association and in 1909 he convened the first White House Conference on the Care of Dependent Children.

Roosevelt brought us the "Square Deal" that domestic program had three basic ideas, conservation of natural resources, control of corporations, and consumer protection. These three demands were referred to as the Three C's, it for helping middle class citizens and attacked plutocracy. you have likely heard the expression "Bust the Trusts" They were predecessors of Today's Big Money Center Banks and Hedge Funds. He protected business from the extreme demands of organized labor.

Roosevelt was a liberal Republican who believed the government was required to regulate social evils such as "the representatives of predatory wealth" who were guilty of "all forms of iniquity from the oppression of wage workers to defrauding the public".

Roosevelt's gave us the eight hour work day, abolished slavery in the Philippines, Improving mine, steamship, railroad, and factory safety, helping the poor from taxation, restricted child labor, and making corporations liable for workers injuries and deaths. He created a National pension system, the predecessor of Social Security. Education and Rural areas were promoted.

He was a true Conservative in my eyes for setting aside land for five National parks and preserved millions and millions of acres of forest and wildlife areas from Alaska to Florida. He built dams and improved waterways. The last remaining Buffalo were saved.

Dwight D (Ike) Eisenhower

Eisenhower was a Liberal powerhouse with a long list of accomplishments not the least of which was the Interstate Highway System which stimulated business throughout the US. Ike took point on the the St. Lawrence Seaway idea, opening up commerce on the great lakes.

Eisenhower spoke of "peace over war" and ended the Korean war. Forced an end to the European invasion into Egypt over the Suez Canal. He liked "Non combat peace keeping missions", and believed and supported the United Nations.

President Eisenhower wanted an end to segregation, saying "I propose to use whatever authority exists in the office of the President to end segregation in the District of Columbia, including the Federal Government, and any segregation in the Armed Forces" he used control of military spending to push the change through, stating "Wherever Federal Funds are expended... , I do not see how any American can justify... a discrimination in the expenditure of those funds." His administration declared racial discrimination a national security issue.

After the Supreme Court Brown v The Board of Education ruling Ike told District of Columbia officials to "make Washington a model for the rest of the country in integrating black and white public school children". When the State of Arkansas refused to integrate their public schools Eisenhower sent in the 101st Airborne to escort and protect students who were to attend Little Rock Central High School. Martin Luther King Jr. even wrote and thanked the President for his actions.

I believe that President Eisenhower's legacy is summed up quite nicely in this statement he to his brother in 1954. "Should any political party attempt to abolish social security, unemployment insurance, and eliminate labor laws and farm programs, you would not hear of that party again in our political history. There is a tiny splinter group, of course, that believes you can do these things. Among them are...a few...Texas oil millionaires, and an occasional politician or business man from other areas. Their number is negligible and they are stupid."

Richard Nixon

Nixon started the Environmental Protection Agency or EPA, the Occupational Safety and Health Administration or OSHA, and in some ways Progressive. He vetoed the Clean Water Act of 1972 and was overridden by Congress on that. He was for health care reform and an Employer Mandate, with government insurance available to all citizens, he called for spending on Cancer as well as signed the the National Sickle Cell Anemia Control Act, yet against legal or decriminalizing of marijuana and other drugs. It was Nixon that started the "War on Drugs" that spent billions of dollars to accomplish very little.

Segregation and busing of black students were in an issue during the Nixon administration he was personally against busing he followed the Supreme Court and Congresses wishes. The first ever Affirmative Action Plan became law under Nixon, and the Philadelphia Plan was signed in 1970. Nixon supported the ERA and appointed many women to government positions, endorsed the Equal Right Amendment which is still currently in the process of state ratification.

Nixon was mostly a moderate on racism and women's rights, here is the kicker, he developed the "Southern Strategy" that used racism in the southern States, as well as other "Conservative"

States to help Republicans win elections by encouraging white people to vote for them.

Nixon moved us out of the Bretton woods agreement and off of the gold standard for the dollar. Experts and novices alike debate scenarios and whether this was ultimately a good or bad thing. At this point it matters not. This "Shock" caused hyper inflation during the 1970s and stagflation after. Many argue that there was not much choice at the time, the gold standard was draining our gold reserves, others argued that we had to move to a floating or fiat currency. This system remains Today, and was the basis for the Euro.

We all know his story ends with his departure over the Watergate scandal. Richard Nixon was the president who's zealous overreach of power set the precedent for all to follow, and the beginning of the paradigm of Conservative rise and Republican hubris. His shenanigans started a "He did it, so I can do it" attitude with future GOP politicians, and that unsaid "Wink" type policy of underlying racism within the party. We see this everyday in the GOP. This was the changing of the old guard, and laid the groundwork for the Modern Republican extreme Conservative rise.

Ronald Reagan

President Ronald Reagan ushered in the new wave of Conservatism in America he was the first of the modern Conservatives who now retains Sainthood for his words and deeds. I remember very clearly him saying at the time that his policies "would be judged by time" and that "we will know in twenty or thirty years if they were good or bad". The jury has currently reached a verdict. While a few of the things he did during his term did help, such as the deregulation and breakup of the old "Ma Bell" Telecommunications industry which gave rise to competition and allowed cell phones to become common and cheap. Reagan's other policies of airline deregulation, bank deregulation, as well as other laissez faire capitalism deregulation especially tax cutting, proved disastrous causing thousands of bankruptcies, multiple recessions, and of course the start of the now monstrous National deficit.

While Reagan had foreign policy successes with a strong defense policy, especially with the fall of the Soviet Union, his domestic and economic policies are now known to be complete failures. Trickle down or supply side economics was nothing more than a giant redistribution of wealth from the middle class and working poor upward to the corporations and the wealthy.

Modified from the original article "8 reasons why Ronald Reagan was the worst president of our lifetime" By Robert Sobel

If you ever happen to come across a Republican on TV lately, you will hear the name Ronald Reagan. Recent Republican debates are a good example of the infatuation that the current Republican party has for Reagan as each candidate name drops the former president at every opportunity. If you only listened to conservatives you would think that Jesus Christ was the only person above Reagan on the totem pole of conservative love. They talk about his love of low taxes, less government and conservative family values. The problem is that when you step out of the conservative dream and come back to reality, you find that not only was Ronald Reagan a bad president, but he was one of the worst presidents we've seen in modern times. Reagan's policies have destroyed the United States for three decades, and for the eight years he was in office, here are eight reasons why Ronald Reagan was a terrible President.

Reagan cut taxes for the Rich, increased taxes on the Middle Class - Ronald Reagan is loved by conservatives and was loved by big business throughout his presidency and there's a reason for it. Under Reagan in January of 1981, the top tax rate was 70%, but when he left office in 1989 the top tax rate was only 28%. Reagan gave all the breaks to all his rich friends, then there was a loss of revenue coming into the federal government. In order to bring revenue back into the government, Reagan had to raise taxes eleven times throughout his time in office. One example was the Tax Equity and Fiscal Responsibility Act of 1982. Reagan raised taxes in seven of the eight years he was in office and the tax increases were felt hardest by the lower and middle class.

Tripled the National Debt - As Reagan cut taxes for the wealthy, the government was left with less money to spend. When Reagan came into office the national debt was $900 billion, by the time he left the national debt had tripled to $2.8 trillion.

Iran/Contra Scandal – It was 1986, Americans hostages were being held by Iranian terrorists. Reagan had a plan to free them by secretly selling guns to, and giving money to Iran. That money went to fund the Nicaragua Contra rebels who were fighting with the Sandinista government of Nicaragua. That was the biggest scandal story in the country, Reagan tried to down play what happened, but his reputation never fully came back.

Reagan Funded Terrorists - The attacks on 9/11 by Al-Qaeda and Osama Bin Laden brought fresh attention to international terrorism. All of a sudden, Americans coast to coast wore their American flag pins, ate their freedom fries and couldn't wait to go to war with anyone who looked like a Muslim. What Americans didn't realize was that the same group that attacked the United States on 9/11 was funded by Ronald Reagan in the 1980s. Prepping for a possible war with the Soviet Union, Ronald Reagan spent billions of dollars funding the Islamist Mujahideen Freedom Fighters in Afghanistan. With billions of American dollars, weapons and training coming their way, the Taliban and Osama Bin Laden took everything they were given and gave it back to the United States over a decade later in the worst possible way.

Unemployment issues - When Ronald Reagan came into office 1981, unemployment was at 7.5%. After Reagan cut taxes for the wealthy, he began raising taxes on the middle and lower class. Corporations started to ship more jobs out of the United States while hiring cheap foreign labor in order to make bigger profit's. While corporations made billions, Americans across the country lost their jobs. As 1982 came to a close, unemployment was nearly 11%. Unemployment began to drop as the years went on, but the jobs that were created were low paying and barely helped people make ends meet. These jobs were termed "McJobs." In honor of minimum wage burger flippers everywhere. The middle and lower class had their wages nearly frozen as the top earners saw dramatic increases in salary.

Ignored the AIDS Epidemic - By the time the 1980s came around, AIDS had become a frightening epidemic. No one understood what AIDS and HIV really was and when people don't understand something, they become scared of it. The fear of AIDS was sweeping across the country and Americans needed a leader to speak out about this virus, that leader never came. Instead of grabbing the bull by the horns and taking charge, Reagan kept quiet. Reagan couldn't even bring himself to say AIDS or HIV until the very last year of his presidency, a leader? Not so much.

Reagan gave amnesty to three million illegal Immigrants so companies could use them as slave labor, In today's GOP, they despise immigrants whether they are legal or not. The biggest reason for undocumented workers coming to the United States is because corporations hire them for cheaper than they would an American. All laws that would crack down on companies who hire undocumented workers have, of course, been removed from any bill.

His attack on Unions and the Middle Class - The Republican war on unions and the middle class has been heating up in states like Wisconsin and Ohio, but it has been going on for a long time. Unions are formed to give a united voice to the workers in an attempt to create fairness between the corporations and their employees. On August 3rd, 1981, PATCO (Professional Air Traffic Controllers Organization) went on strike in an effort to get better pay and safer working conditions. Taking the side of the corporations, Ronald Reagan unlawfully fired over 11,000 workers for not returning to work.

Deregulation of Banks – Deregulation of the financial industry directly led to, or contributed to three US Recessions 1990-1991, 2000-2001, 2007-2008, And the Savings and Loan crisis when more than 1,000 banks failed in 1988 and 1989, at an average rate of 2 per day, for over two years. According to the FDIC 1,502 banks failed under Reagan's terms, and over 1,300 more in the next 4 years. 9 of the 10 largest banks in Texas failed. During the 1980s 7 out of 8 of the US Money Center Banks were underwater or insolvent. They were quietly funded by the Fed during this time. Since that time there have been hundreds of mergers and consolidations thus creating the now "Too Big To Fail" banks. In 1981, Fannie Mae issued it's first mortgage pass through and the mortgage backed security was born, these products directly caused the Great recession of 2007-2008.

Deregulation of the Airlines caused multiple National and International carriers to go bankrupt. Pan-Am, Eastern, TWA, etc... more than 42 airlines have filed bankruptcy since 1980 and Reagan's deregulation. there is a marked diminishing of safety and oversight, and service has been paired back to smaller locals. Consolidation of smaller companies being swallowed up by the more powerful has been the norm.

During the 1980s when Iraq was at war with Iran, Iraq used Siren gas and Mustard gas against the northern Kurds. The Kurdish are Iraqis that live in the Northern Iraq mountain region. Imagine that! Iraq used nerve gas against it's own people. The US knew all about it, President Reagan Knew, the CIA knew, the US Military knew. We did nothing. We told no one. Why? Because we were Iraq's ally in that war. Does anyone besides me feel that the US is a bit hypocritical here? A CIA document that was declassified recently of US Military report on the matter stated that "Nerve gas was a good tool for the Iraqis to help win tough battles." I just want to point out that this was just another covered up Republican regime atrocity. The man who led the attacks was Hassan al-Majid a first cousin of Saddam

Hussein. These events killed more than 100,000 people, Pretty much sanctioned at the time by the US. President Reagan was a terrible President.

Ronald Reagan "Benghazi" type attacks that nobody sad a word about;

October 23, 1983. the US Embassy in Beirut was attacked and 299 people were killed, 241 Americans. This attack was the worst day for the United States Marine Corps since World War II's Battle at Iwo Jima. Reagan's response was to Cut and Run out of Lebanon.

On December 12, 1983. The US embassy in Kuwait was attacked by a suicide truck bomber. This act of terror killed 6 people in total, 5 of which were Americans. Yet, the weak President Reagan refused to call it an Act of Terror. he never even put out an official statement condemning it.

September 20, 1984. Hezbollah used a truck bomb to kill 24 people.

November 1984. A car bomb killed 1 at the US Bogota Columbia Embassy.

Right Wing Conservatives

The Conservative/Republican Agenda

Cutting Taxes for the Wealthy and the Corporations. "ReCon's" have used a number of lies to convince Americans that they have the fiscal answers. Supply side economics, Trickle down theory, Privatization, Deregulation, and of course Tax Cuts increase tax revenue and create jobs. All of these are Myths, nothing more.

Supply Side Economics just creates consumer bubbles that are unsustainable. If we as a world continue to cut down trees, rape the earth for every last metal, mineral, and fossil fuel, what happens when the earth runs out? The folly that we can just keep using and using, producing disposable products, marketing them to the masses, and ultimately throwing them away thereby creating an ever increasing waste stream and ever growing pollution problem amounts to the greatest lie ever told.

Trickle down theory is a bold face lie that has never worked, never will work, and never even had any chance of working. Everyone has heard the old saying "The Rich get richer and the poor get poorer" is true. Wealthy people and corporations have absolutely no reason to ever re-invest, or create a single job, it is antithetical to human behavior. In reality the more wealth and power accumulated the more likely of worker exploitation.

Privatization is just a way for corporations to take something done by the government and charge the government more to do the same thing. There is not a single example of privatization that has ever saved one red cent. Again and again we have seen contractors take over things for the government, Military Buildings, security, even supplying food for the troops. Prisons are another example. These contracts have made hundreds of billions for the companies that are awarded them, costs increasing over and over again, and never once saved a nickel. The ReCon's would have us believe that the Post Office, Medicare, Medicaid, The IRS, and Social Security would be better run in the hands of for profit corporations when in fact the opposite is always true. The government is always more efficient and less expensive even with the known waste and abuse.

Deregulation of the banking and investment industry has caused many recessions and the destruction of large amounts of wealth, mostly of the middle and lower class. Lack of good industrial oversight destroys our environment and peoples lives on a daily basis. Oil wells that blow out and pollute or waterways, pipelines that constantly leak, financial instruments designed to cheat whomever buys them. After the great depression this country had a period of over sixty years without a major recession. Since deregulation began we have had on average two per decade a series of booms and busts, where it always seems the wealthy boom, and the rest of us go bust every five years or so.

Tax cuts have never created a single job, and have actually been a majority of the reason we have large deficit's. If Bush had not signed those tax cuts for the wealthy into law, the deficit would have been paid down to zero by 2008. During that same time we had negative job creation, the largest off shoring of jobs to other countries and the slowest period of wage growth. Literally a 100% failure rate. ReCon's still cling to this idea as the backbone of their fiscal prudence. Here is a novel idea, if you actually want to pay down the deficit then we have to raise taxes on someone, somewhere. We must increase revenue. That is the reality that nobody wants to believe or hear.

Class Warfare - There is absolutely a class war going on here in the US. It is so clear that even the simplest of minds can understand it. Wages have not increased in forty years, minimum wage has been stagnant. Healthcare costs have been transferred from the company to the worker. The cost of consumer goods and service has steadily increased, Housing as well. Yet somehow the companies have enjoyed increased profit's and growth. Their stock prices have gone up dramatically. CEOs and all the other officers and board members have had huge increases in salary, bonuses and benefit's and all off of the sweat of the workers brow. Workers have had to subsidize their own existence with loans, home equity and/or credit card and personal loans. Student loans to put their kids through college. All the while the wealthy have seen their income rise and rise and rise. The net worth of the middle class, the working poor and the poor have dwindled lower and lower. We are now at a point where the top 20% control 80% of the money and the bottom 40% control 0.03% of the money. Ultimately the ReCon's aim is to make debt slaves of all of us and have an unlimited supply of super cheap labor for generations.

Advancing Extreme Christian Laws, Racism, Bigotry and Misogyny.

Ever since Saint Reagan got in bed with the Christian Right, ReCon's have moved further and further right pandering to Ignorance and superstition. Their mission in life is crystal clear. Anti Abortion, Anti-homosexuality, Anti-Adultery, oh wait that one is a ReCon Favorite, Anti-Contraception, Anti-Pornography, Anti-Gambling, unless of course it's Wall Street doing the gambling with our money, Forcing Creationism, Christian Prayer, and Abstinence only into our Schools. Of particular note here is that while they are fervently against Muslim Sharia Law, Christian Law is exactly the same as Sharia Law. They argue that it is absolutely not, because the penalties are different. This is not true according to the book of Leviticus, the penalties are exactly the same, death for all violations. Then they say only go according to the New Testament. OK, so then according to the Book of John the penalty is also death. Sharia Law is in fact, Christian Law, period. Furthermore ReCon's then twist Christianity to pass laws that actually harm the poor even more economically, the sick by withholding access to healthcare, the elderly, minorities, and of course women. The hypocrisy is so overwhelming I want to vomit. Examples of this are that they cut social programs like SNAP and Welfare, attack Medicare and Medicaid, Social Security all the while ever-increasing the Military budget. Exactly the opposite of what Jesus taught. You can not praise the Lord and pass the ammunition. Another example is being pro-life and for the death penalty. You are either pro-life or you are not, you can not pick as you wish without compromising the underlying principle. One can not be an Ayn Rand 'Rugged Individual" and Christian at the same time, it's one OR the other.

Voter Suppression - Now that the Conservative

stacked Supreme Court has struck down article 4 of the Voting Act of 1964 in effect Deregulating States voters law. Many Southern States have wasted no time in pushing through new laws that are in fact old laws originally struck down in the 1960s these were known as "Jim Crow" Laws that were blatantly unfair to blacks, minorities, and the poor. Several States including Texas and North Carolina, Alabama have passed laws redistricting or Gerrymandering their State districts to give ReCon's the upper hand to be able to win elections while only receiving just a minority of the vote. Voting can be skewed 10% - 15% against them and they technically will still win. Voter ID laws directly affect a larger percentage of Blacks, Minorities, Women, and a new demographic, the youth vote. All of these targeted demographics vote overwhelmingly Liberal and Democrat. I believe that ReCon's can not win election based on their policies and ideas and must now resort to legislative tricks and voter suppression to keep office. Democracy be damned.

Promotion of War - ReCon's never met a war or a Police Action that they didn't like. Or a gun sale for that matter. It fuels the profit's of the Industrial Military Complex. War profiteering pure and simple. Ever wonder why we are constantly at war with someone or something? Terrorists, Drugs, Crime, Iraq, Iran, Kuwait, Syria? The new war is the war on illegal immigrants, which is a Cunard because currently we have zero inflows. That won't stop the ReCon's from spending zillions on fences, drones, surveillance and warm pulses to "Secure" the border. This will not stop until we have jet fighters and tanks and every other half trillion dollar military contract product patrolling the Rio Grande. After that they will find a way to get us entangled in Syria and Iran. This is why we can never have peace, we are permanently at war with straw men.

The lies just keep coming and coming. Laws designed by groups like ALEC and the Heritage Foundation to "Fix" non-existent problems. Laws to combat Voter fraud that actually defrauds voters. Pro Gun laws that make us less safe. Increased Military spending and citizens rights stripped all in the name of "National Security" The constant expenditure of US Treasure be it money or lives all for profit's. Let's be real clear here... The Republican Party prays to the Almighty Dollar and uses religion to convince the ignorant that they are righteous. The reality is that they are Vile Anti-Christian haters intent on imposing their iron will onto the rest of us. The people must fight against them, vote against them, and argue against them as hard as we possibly can to insure that the United States remains Free and continue to be a beacon of hope, for all people to better themselves and their children's lives for the future.

Some Right Wing Myths

Do any of you know personally, or are, a woman who actually had an abortion in her 3rd trimester to fit into a particular dress OR to go on a cruise OR because she got tired of being pregnant? I have never met one. I believe that none of you have either. So all of those 3rd trimester abortions that the Republicans keep talking about don't really exist. It's all Just Conservative bullshit.

Do any of you know personally, or are, a person who's marriage is or was threatened by any gay person? The sanctity of the institution of marriage challenged solely by an individual seeking to be married to the person they love? Again, I have never met one. I believe that none of you have either. So all of this talk about the sanctity of marriage being threatened by homosexuality is a lie. Republicans keep talking about what doesn't really exist. It's all Just Conservative bullshit.

Do any of you know personally, or are, a rich person or corporation that runs a business in America who got rich without using any of the following; public roads, public schools, the internet, electricity, telephones, Government contracts, or anything invented by NASA (yes this includes Velcro), a bank loan backed by the

FDIC, or paper money? And if you actually do find an example of this one, a bonus prize for any business that fit's the previous qualifications that pays their workers such that none of them need to use food stamps. I do not know of any such person or business. I believe that none of you do either. Just another example of Conservative bullshit.

I am tired of the lies and bigotry promoted in this Country. If you are going to argue these points, then have some damn proof that they exist. The same can be said of voter fraud, religious persecution, abortions causing cancer, doctors infringing on 2nd Amendment rights, Lower taxes creating jobs, The post office contributing to the countries debt, Social Security being insolvent, and just about every other Right wing talking point.

All of this crap is being made into political hay to distract you from the reality that The Republicans are responsible for most of the Deficit. The deficit grew the most under Reagan, GH Bush, and GW Bush. They have ruined the economy with their policies that don't work. All so they can keep cutting taxes for the rich and their corporate friends. That is their main agenda, and will continue to be so. War profiteering and the proliferation of religious ideology into our government is their secondary agenda. This is what is destroying America. Corruption and lies. Not Liberals.

I just love how Conservatives think. Their logic kind of reminds me of a comedy act. For 40 years all I remember hearing is those "stupid" Liberals... I put forth the idea that it is, in fact, the Conservatives that are the stupid ones... Here let me give you some examples;

Conservatives all preach about making people take "Personal Responsibility" and never say a thing about "Corporate Responsibility" like when an oil company has a pipeline spill, or when an oil well blows up. Conservatives give them a free ride, because as "They" all know you can not hold any "Job Creators' responsible for anything. After all, we don't want them to stop creating all of those so called "jobs". Then they double down by legislating corporations huge tax subsidies, then they triple down by lowering their tax rates, In reality the Corporations are laughing so hard coffee is coming out of their noses. Squirreling more money in offshore tax havens. Keeping off shore profit's out of the US to avoid taxes. They pay Ginormous salaries and bonuses to their board members and top executives, so as to reduce their tax liability even more. Then to add insult to injury they freeze workers wages, make them pay for larger portions of their health plans. Lay off US workers and hire cheap slave labor from God only knows where. then they subcontract to Companies from cheaper Countries. It reminds me of the old joke about "Business Ethics", there are none.

Conservatives are all against "Welfare" and they hold up Ronald Reagan's "Welfare Queens" as the shining example of how unjust it is to the working man. Yet they support most severely "Corporate Welfare" in all it's forms. Oil subsidies in the tens of billions of dollars for Exxon, Chevron, Conoco, Shell, Marathon, etc... and God Forbid we should cut tax breaks for corporate jets. After all we wouldn't want all those super rich CEOs to go without. Seems to me rather than letting poor or sick people out to dry, we should put profitable corporations out instead. The deflection here is unbelievable, They shout and scream like the Wizard of Oz about the millions we spend on welfare programs all the while letting tens of Billions out the door for corporations. Heads I win, tails you lose...

Conservatives believe if we give more money to the wealthy and the Corporations, that will give them incentive to work harder, create jobs, and expand their businesses. However, if we give more money to the poor they will just get lazy, do nothing, and want more money. Wait? What? So let me get this straight. We have given more and more money to the wealthy and the corporations and they got lazy and wanted more? And the poor wanted less? Or is it the vessel with the pestle has the poison, and the chalice from the palace has the brew that is true, or is it the vessel from the palace has the... well you see the problem...

Conservatives say that if we get rid of minimum wage, child labor laws, safety regulation, Unions, etc... that will create more jobs and somehow allow workers to make more money. Right to work laws create jobs. Insert fox guarding hen house joke here...

Conservatives all want mandatory drug testing for any type of government help like unemployment, welfare, food stamps, WIC, Snap, etc... And they don't care how much it costs to do that. They did this in Florida, and it cost them $60 million dollars to save $2 million dollars. I swear, you can't make this stuff up. Using that one state example and expanding on that program would cost taxpayers $3 BILLION dollars to save $100 MILLION. Brilliant! Only a Conservative mind can wrap itself around that concept. This reminds me of the two partners that make widgets, and the one partner says to the other "Hey if it cost 50 cents to make each widget, and we sell them for a quarter won't we lose money"? The other partner replied "Nah, we will make it up in volume"...

I said earlier that Conservative logic reminds me of a comedy act, I didn't say it was any good... Ba Dump Bump...

Conservatives have been Judge, Jury and Executioner of Liberals for the last Fifty years. They have looked down the end of their nose at us, and demand that we follow their ideas blindly no matter how ridiculous they are. Their Policies have not only destroyed this county, they are steeped in Lies, Superstition, and Fear. They have called us every name in the book, from Stupid, Elite, Godless, Ignorant, Morons, Hippies, Dirty, Perverts, etc... They must be right because they have God and the Bible on their side... They are truly Hateful Bigots, Misogynists, and Racists. Conservatives condemn and fear anyone who is not exactly like them. They suppress women and minorities. They suppress our votes through intimidation and illegal legislation. They force their religious views on the rest of us. Then when we point out these flaws they turn and call us the Close Minded Hypocrites... They truly believe that 90% of Americans think exactly like they do, when in fact the exact opposite is true. They create imaginary Bogeymen to scare us, Welfare Queens, Terrorists, Junkies, Communists, and Socialists. They spend and spend our Tax dollars like water and blame it on us. They believe that they are above the law while we are to be prosecuted.

And watch how they will take everything said here, and use it against whoever posts this... Just like a little child in a school yard that says "I know you are, but what am I?" I believe it is time to treat Conservatives like the little children that they are.

Gun control is actually a conservative ideal. A liberal or laissez faire government would allow people to buy and own whatever they wanted. An actual conservative government would take them away, whatever the justification. For example, a liberal government would be OK with murder, and just fine with retribution.

A conservative government will tax it's citizens more in order to provide the people with services. While services are good to have, an abundance of government services tends to remove a lot of personal choice from the citizens. A liberal government would allow people to allocate funds how they like, and seek the services or care they wanted.

If the government noses into your business, it's conservative. If it doesn't, then it's liberal.

Historically Conservative Ideals
Conservation of any natural resource
Making no changes, leaving the status quo
Regression to a simpler time

Embracing tradition

Facts that drive Conservatives absolutely nuts;

9/11 happened on George W. Bush's watch, therefore he did NOT keep America safe.

A Socialist wrote the Pledge of Allegiance.

Abortion is a relevant medical procedure, just ask Rick Santorum.

Africa is the birthplace of the human race.

America is a nation of immigrants, so in fact, we are all anchor babies.

Barack Obama is the first black President, get over it.

Barack Obama gave the order killing Osama Bin Laden. It took him two and half years to do what Bush couldn't get done in eight.

Bush held freaking hands with the King of Saudi Arabia.

Churches should stay out of politics, or be taxed. That's the law.

Corporations are NOT people. People are people.

Corporations care more about profit's than they do about people.

Democrats take care of the sick. Republicans take their credit cards and then deny them medical attention.

Dinosaurs walked the Earth before Jesus did.

Evolution is real.

Federal law trumps state law.

Fox News is owned by an Australian and has a Saudi prince as an investor.

Fox News isn't real news, it's just a racist, sexist, hateful, right-wing propaganda machine. In fact they won a lawsuit in the Florida courts that they are allowed to report incorrect news as entertainment. News Corp who owns FOX News is considered an entertainment company.

Getting out of a recession requires government spending.

Global warming is real.

"God" is a particle called Higgs-Boson.

Greed is one of the seven deadly sins, and

Republicans love it.

Hate is not a Christian value.

Health care is a Right, not a product for sale.

I think, therefore, I am not Republican.

Jesus had dark skin and did not speak English.

Jesus healed the sick, helped the poor, and for free.

Jesus was a Liberal.

Labor unions helped build America.

Michael Moore is the greatest documentary film maker of all time.

Muslims are protected by the Constitution, just like Christians are.

Paying your taxes is patriotic.

President Obama saved the American auto manufacturing industry, Republicans want to destroy it.

Public schools educate all children. Private schools indoctrinate children.

Reagan legalized abortion as Governor of California.

Reagan raised taxes eleven times as President.

Reagan was president of a labor union.

Reagan saved Social Security.

Reagan supported gun control.

Republican politicians love their government-run health care.

Republicans are hypocrites.

Republicans complain about immigrants taking American jobs, then freely give American jobs to foreigners overseas.

Republicans controlled government in the 1920's, lowered taxes on the wealthy, and caused the Great Depression; now they've done it again.

Republicans don't want to pay for your birth control, but they want you to pay for their Viagra.

Republicans hate illegal immigrants, unless they need their lawns mowed or their houses cleaned.

Republicans have their own terrorists, just look up Timothy McVeigh.

Republicans invaded Iraq for oil, so Iraq should be allowed to invade Texas to get it back.

Republicans love outsourcing, just ask the Chinese Communists.

Republicans only care about children before they are born.

Republicans say teachers are union thugs, then proceed to rape and mug the entire middle class on behalf of corporations.

Republicans spend more money than Democrats.

Republicans think rape isn't a crime, but miscarriages are.

Republicans are Anti-Gay Marriage, Pro-Lesbian sex.

Republicans have pushed the same failed economic policies since 1880.

Roe v. Wade was a bipartisan ruling made by a conservative leaning Supreme Court.

Separation of church and state is part of the Constitution, it's called the First Amendment.

Social Security is solvent through 2038.

The Christian-Right boycotts movies that have violence, and then promotes guns and insurrection.

The Civil War was about slavery, not state's rights.

The Constitution is the law, not the Bible.

The current corporate tax rate is the lowest in 60 years, so stop whining about it being too high.

The Earth is 4.54 billion years old, not 6,000.

The Founding Fathers were liberals and supported socialized medicine.

The Oval Office is not a "whites only" office.

President Obama is not a Muslim.

The President's name is Barack Hussein Obama and he was born in the United States.

The Republican answer to the oil spill was to apologize to BP, a foreign oil company.

The South lost the Civil War, get over it.

The white race isn't disappearing, it's evolving.

Voter disenfranchisement is immoral and Anti-American, that's why Republicans do it.

When Republicans see black, they attack.

Women are equal citizens who deserve equal rights.

Women control their own bodies.

Yay! Wing Nut Glenn Beck is no longer on FOX.

Bottom line? If you want to piss off a Conservative, just tell them the truth.

Drug Testing

Drug Testing is wrong for a couple of reasons. First it is a direct invasion of privacy and therefore unconstitutional, and a violation of the Fourth Amendment. The idea that people collecting welfare or food stamps are all on drugs is a myth, an untruth, a canard. This whole concept is born out of the Ronald Reagan "Welfare Queen" propaganda. I simply do not understand why people keep bringing this up again, and again. There is unequivocal proof that drug testing is a worthless idea and would in fact cost States and the Federal Government Billions with no benefit. Governor Rick Scott in Florida had his Republican legislature pass a mandatory drug testing bill. (of course his Brother in law got the contract) yet the results are astounding, The Miami Herald Newspaper published the results, it cost the State of Florida well over $2.2 Million Dollars to test all of their welfare recipients and they found that 2.6% tested positive, mostly for marijuana. Ah! Ha! you say. See? I told you. Well, there ya go. But wait, not so fast my Conservative and Republican Brainiacs, because the net amount of money that the State saved by not paying that 2.6% of moochers was only $45,780. Overall this experiment was a complete and utter failure, Florida threw $2 Million dollars away and saved absolutely nothing. If all States adopted this ridiculous idea Nationwide it would cost the Country over $2.5 Billion Dollars. So the concept is penny wise and pound foolish. Furthermore Each State will have to spend additional millions to defend all of the inevitable lawsuit's that will follow. Florida has to now defend itself against lawsuit's from the ACLU, as well as private citizens. There is no assurance that the State will win the case, or that an appeal, or the Supreme Court will side with them either. All of those legal fees must be paid by the State. Can you can explain how spending Billions of dollars to theoretically save Thousands can make any sense to anyone, I would be happy to change my mind. There is always some fraud in Charity. Let us suppose for a minute that when Jesus performed the miracle of the seven loaves and fish, a few people there might have already had something to eat? Should Jesus have tested the masses to see if any of them had drank wine? Would Jesus have not given bread and fish to those few as well? The concept of drug testing for any reason is Anti American according to the US Constitution and quite Anti Christian according to the Bible. Now let me really blow your mind with a crazy fact, more than half of the recipients of welfare and food stamps are young children. Do you really think six year old's should be drug tested? Now do you see the absurdity of the whole idea of drug testing?

The Religious Right

Religion is Terrorism, go to any church and they will tell you that if you do not follow their teachings "You will be damned and burn in hell fire for eternity". This is supposed to scare you into submission. The exact definition of terrorism.

If a police officer threatened your child with being burned if they are not good, it would be considered abuse. Why do we tolerate the same threat from our Religions?

Some Christian fundamentalist Republicans believe that the "Care Bears" turn children gay, and perhaps make them vulnerable to witchcraft.

Massachusetts State Senate candidate Sandi Martinez, who believes, among other things, that the Smurfs and Care Bears are turning Our Children into witches.

According to the Lowell Sun and the Boston Globe, Martinez embraces beliefs surrounding right-wing Christianity. Martinez once hosted an access TV show where she has proclaimed that 1980s children's shows such as "The Smurfs" and "The Care Bears" can lure children into witchcraft which, according to candidate Martinez, is promoted in public schools.
On her cable TV show in 2004, Martinez warned

that going "Trick or Treating, Harry Potter books, and the new age images" presented in 1980s TV programming like "The Smurfs" and "The Care Bears" could "De-stigmatize the occult and leave children vulnerable to the lure of witchcraft."

Our Pledge of Allegiance and the Myth of "One Nation Under God" Modified from original article published April 27, 2013 By Allen Clifton

You hear so many on the right claim that our country was founded on Christianity. This is a "Christian Nation" they proclaim. They use the Pledge of Allegiance as "proof" that this nation was founded as a Christian nation. Many of them put bumper stickers on their vehicles that say "One Nation Under GOD!" or emphasize the word "God" when they recite our nation's pledge.

It all sounds great, except, our pledge wasn't written until until 1892. Yes, you read that correctly, the Pledge of Allegiance was written one hundred and sixteen years after the Revolutionary War and Declaration of Independence.

Not just that, the phrase "Under God" wasn't even in the original pledge.

"I pledge allegiance to my Flag and the Republic for which it stands, one nation, indivisible, with liberty and justice for all."

And it gets better. The author of the pledge was a Christian socialist named Francis Bellamy, He stood for workers rights and believed in an equal distribution of economic resources. He believed in the nationalization of certain industries, because he feared their manipulation and corruption in the hands of a private sector which would put profit's before people.

So a Christian minister wrote the pledge, and didn't include the word "God" or "Christian" and to add insult to injury, he was a socialist. I'm sure by now most conservatives reading this will have already decided I'm making all of this up. But oh, there's more.

In 1923, some more text was added to the pledge.

"I pledge allegiance to the Flag of the United States of America and to the Republic for which it stands, one nation, indivisible, with liberty and justice for all."

Thirty one years after it's written the pledge still didn't contain the phrase "under God."

In fact, it wasn't until 1954 that the phrase "under God" was actually added to the pledge, because people were so afraid of Godless communism in the time of Joe McCarthy.

"I pledge allegiance to the flag of the United States of America, and to the republic for which it stands, one nation, under God, indivisible, with liberty and justice for all."

Sixty two years after it's creation did the pledge finally include the words "under God."

I can already hear some now, "But our currency has "In God We Trust" written on it! It's our nation's motto!"

That's true, it does and it is. But "In God We Trust" didn't appear on any currency until 1864. In fact the motto "In God We Trust" wasn't even adopted into this country officially until 1956 and didn't appear on our paper currency until 1957. It was only on our coins up to that point.

Then let's not forget that the only reference to religion in our Bill of Rights is in our First Amendment, which states:

"Congress shall make no law respecting an establishment of religion, or prohibiting the free exercise thereof; or abridging the freedom of speech, or of the press; or the right of the people peaceably to assemble, and to petition the Government for a redress of grievances."

The word "Christianity" doesn't appear even once in our Constitution.

So when these people proudly boast about our nation being a "Christian Nation" or that we were a nation founded "under God," remind them of these facts.

Because the more they press the issue, the more they think you're simply making all of this up, the more they continue to insist this country was founded on Christianity and use our currency or pledge as proof...

The more they display their ignorance of our history, of reality and prove that they would rather believe a lie than know the truth.

This is in response to a Facebook post from Sue;

Hey Sue, you certainly have the right to your opinion. Some of your statements are a bit perplexing, for instance if we look back at the original intentions of our forefathers in creating the Declaration of Independence and the Bill of Rights, what do you think we would see? I have read all of those documents many times and have studied the history of most of the founding fathers. First of all most of them were Deists that believed in reason over religion, they believed in secular government and many wrote statements saying so. Jefferson in his letter to the Danbury Baptists and Madison in the Treaty of Tripoli.

You call our Legal system a "So called Legal System" I take it that you are against Justice? Perhaps you would like to replace it with something of your own design? Exactly what current laws are not being enforced? Should we prosecute more offenses and put more people in prison at $65,000 per person per year? Who will pay for that? You?

You think BP has actually cleaned up the Gulf? Why then is there a giant "dead spot" for hundreds of miles where they "sunk" the oil with all of that toxic dispersant?

You say you hate "Socialized" medicine, yet offer no explanation why our medical system is in shambles, 37th in the world behind every other developed nation? France and Germany have the best and second best medical services and doctors in the world, they cover 100% of everyone and do it for approximately $6,500 per person, In America millions go without any coverage whatsoever and it costs us over $16,500 per person. It never ceases to amaze me how people who do not even understand what Socialized, Socialism, and Democratic Socialism actually mean, but they are against it. Even if it's better? The Right is actually trying to convince people to not buy health insurance from the exchanges under Obamacare. Really? We should pay double from a private company, or have no insurance at all? That's so much better.

(sarcasm) You work in a "free clinic" and that gives you the right to judge all of the patients that come in? And your jealous of what they have? Seriously? If we adopted a Socialized Healthcare system, you would get free medical too.

Last week the employment statistics were 18 million unemployed and 4 million available jobs. Please explain how the 14 million people who there are no jobs for are lazy? Exactly what jobs should they take? Maybe they should take yours? You are parroting the Reagan Welfare Queen propaganda that we have all heard a thousand times. it's a myth, all the while corporations like Exxon that made 45 Billion in profit's are paying 11% in taxes, getting billions in government subsidies, and have been off shoring money and jobs for decades? Just the lost tax revenue from Exxon alone would be enough to pay for the entire Welfare and SNAP programs in the US. Correct me if I am wrong, but I thought that Jesus taught us to heal the sick, feed the poor and hungry, clothe the naked, etc... It's not very "Christian" of us to cut that out, now is it? You probably shouldn't "Covet" the things that they have, I believe it's one of the 10 Commandments, and a sin. Please point out exactly what part, article, and clause prohibits a person from having a child out-of-wedlock?
Currently there is nobody coming to America, we have net negative immigration. Expatriation is at

an all time high and increasing month by month. So who exactly is getting what for free?

I am Christian and quite pro choice. it's real simple while I may, or may try to influence my family on personal beliefs, I would never presume to force my beliefs upon another. If you are Pro life and choose to not have an abortion, fine, don't get one, if you choose to not use contraception, fine again, don't use any. Do not presume to force your belief system an another citizen. Currently zero Federal money is used for abortions in this country, that is the law of the land. Anyone telling you otherwise is simply misinformed. If a female soldier is raped and wants an abortion, she should be able to get one and the Government should pay for it as she is entitled to healthcare in exchange for service. Not so currently. Do you agree with that? I am sick to death that my tax money is used to build weapons of war that kill hundreds of thousands and there is nothing I can do about it, your moaning about your tax money being used to fund a few abortions and some contraceptives? Which is the greater sin the murder of masses? Or the "murder" of a few?

Sharia Law vs Christian Law

Let us compare Muslim Sharia law and Christian law. I say they are one and the same. Devout Christians say that I am nuts, that may be true, but that doesn't mean I am incorrect. Decide for yourself.

Muslims believe a woman must stay a virgin until she is married and Christians believe a woman must stay a virgin until she is married.

Muslims believe adultery is a sin and Christians believe adultery is a sin.

Muslims believe abortion is a sin and Christians believe abortion is a sin.

Muslims believe pornography is a sin and Christians believe pornography is a sin.

Muslims believe homosexuality is a sin and Christians believe homosexuality is a sin.

Muslims believe contraception is a sin and Christians believe contraception is a sin.

Muslims believe gambling is a sin and Christians believe gambling is a sin.

Muslims use water for purification and Christians use water for purification.

Muslims have obligatory prayer and
Christians believe you must pray each day.

Muslims worship at at a Mosque and
Christians worship at at a Church.

Muslims pay alms and Christians pay tithes.

Muslims fast during Ramadan and
Christians fast during Lent.

Muslims pilgrimage to Mecca and
Christians pilgrimage to the Vatican and
Jerusalem.

Muslims believe drinking alcohol is a sin and
Christians believe drinking alcohol is a sin.

Muslims believe Allah's law should be above all
Christians believe God's law should be above all.

OK, I give up... What's the freaking difference?
Both want to control you, your money and your
sex life. Change the Law of the land to their laws.
And inflict their beliefs on you. America is a
Secular Country. The Constitution was written
that way on purpose by the founding fathers.
Separation of Church and State protects all
Religions, and Non-Believers alike. Christian law
is no better than Sharia law for our Constitution.
Speak up for Separation of Church and State
or convert...

Only Muslims can be Terrorists?

People made such a big deal calling the Boston Bombers "Islamic Terrorists" Here is a list of "Christian Terrorists" so Bigots can tell the difference. We can even call some of them "Catholic Terrorists" if you want. Why not just call them "Terrorists" and be done with it?

Richard Paplawski
James Von Brunn
John Patrick Bedell
Andrew Joseph Stack
Jared Loughner
Daniel Cowart
Anders Behring Brevik
Byron Williams
Ted Kacznski
Timothy McVeigh
Scott Philip Roeder
Terry Nichols

Remember Ireland and the Irish Republican Army or IRA? They bombed, and bombed, and bombed... Surely they were terrorists.

I call out Conservative and Republican bull crap as completely Anti Christian.

Jesus Christ taught us "Charity toward the least fortunate as a sign of compassion and the ability to earn everlasting life". Christ felt that helping the poor was so important, that he gave instructions to the rich to sell all their belongings and hand the proceeds to the poor, but it is blatantly obvious to me that his message is completely lost on Republicans.

1st John 3:17 says "Whoever has earthly possessions and notices a brother in need and yet withholds his compassion from him, how can the love of God be present in him"?

Jesus said "I tell you the truth, it is hard for a rich man to enter the kingdom of heaven. Again I tell you, it is easier for a camel to go through the eye of a needle than for a rich man to enter the kingdom of God" The Bible has this in two places, once in Mark 10:25 and again in Luke 18:25.

I do not understand why Republicans wish to follow Ayn Rand's fiction about rugged individualism, after all she was a Russian Atheist who spent a good amount of her life on government benefit's. Ayn Rand wrote "Achievement of your happiness is the only moral purpose of your life, and that happiness, not pain or mindless self-indulgence, is the proof of your moral integrity, since it is the proof and the result of your loyalty to the achievement of your values." Christianity and Jesus tells us the opposite. In Matthew 22:39 "You shall love your neighbor as yourself." in Matthew 5:42 "Give to the one who begs from you, and do not refuse the one who would borrow from you." and John 13:34 "A new commandment I give to you, that you love one another just as I have loved you, you also are to love one another." The fiction of Ayn Rand is an exact opposite of Christian teaching.

Jesus and his disciples spoke strongly and many times against exploitation of workers and of the poor. This should be part and parcel of being "Pro Life", but these are low priority in the Republican party. Other than Abortion, Republican ideology is made up of primarily Anti Life stances, or should I say mostly pro death?

The Apostle Paul said "Greed is equal to idolatry, and the love of money is the root of all evils". Republicans promote greed and worship profit's above every other value. In fact they honor these moral errors.

Peter warned against malice and slander. Republican leaders do not confront and reject, rather they support popular slanderers who promote their agenda.

The Mormon and Catholic organizations both have massive wealth they could share with the needy as Christ commanded, but instead they hide behind non profit status and lobby for more tax cuts for the wealthy. Jesus said would they have difficulty entering into the kingdom of God.

Many Republicans are notorious religious hypocrites, they claim they hold up the Christian ethic while they work relentlessly to punish the poor with every damn piece of legislation and every single budget proposal they endorse. Republicans are absolutely 100% Anti Christian.

Biblical Definitions of Marriage

I thought I would drop this little tid-bit in for clarification for those that continually say that the biblical definition of marriage is one man and one woman. While that may be true here are some other biblical definitions of marriage.

One man and his Sister
One man and his dead brothers wife
One man and his rape victim
One man and many women
One man and 700 women and 300 concubines
One man and one woman and her slaves
One soldier and his virgin prisoners

Someone had posted out that prayer is no longer allowed in school in any way, shape or form.

Let us get our facts straight. Prayer is allowed in school, however it can not be led, introduced, or directed by administration or teachers. Individual students can and do pray all the time, especially before tests. I went to a Public High School and we had a "Prayer Club" it was after school hours and student directed. Football teams and other sports teams break off into a group, take a knee and pray before every game. Students who wish to take part do, and those that do not wish to, do not. Generally the Coach will give a time for this activity and may take part. He just can not schedule it, or make it mandatory. Conversely, if a student is Humanist or Atheist they do not have to say "Under God" in the pledge, or take part in any thing they believe is objectionable based on their religion. The founding Fathers intentionally left out mention of religion on purpose. Their intent was that Religious belief is between citizens and their conscience. That morality has worked perfectly. There have been incursions, in the 1950's "Red Scare" where many Churches and Right Wing politicians added Christian ideology onto our money and into our pledge as a way of combating those "Godless" Communists. In reality, that is baseless, however Fear of Communism was used to help swing the pendulum to the right. We probably should repeal all of those Red Scare laws as they serve no purpose in our Government.

This Country went to war for independence over the concept of "Taxation Without Representation" but how do we feel about the opposite? There is a group of people in this Country that are quite active within our political system, they lobby and spend money to support candidates and take out huge ads on billboards, newspapers, magazines. They have their own websites and community groups that go out and canvas people and try to influence their votes and donations. Yet these people pay no taxes.
Republicans are always talking about "Expanding

the Tax Base" and that more "moochers" who pay nothing should pay their fair share. The people that I am talking about here have a tax exempt status that is predicated on them being non political. I would call these groups "Highly Represented Without Taxation". They all pay absolutely zero Federal, State or Local Taxes.

They are trying to bring about the equivalent of Sharia Law to our Constitution. They say that they want to change the US Constitution to force everyone to follow their beliefs. They lobby for the government intervention of Woman's rights. They want to force their ideology into our schools and textbooks. They don't believe in Science or Public Education. You know who I am talking about but maybe you think they are harmless.

The group I speak of here is the Christian Right which is made up of The Evangelical Christians, mostly Southern Baptists, The Catholic Church, Mormons and The Church of Jesus Christ of Latter day Saints or LDS Church. The Religious Right also includes Muslims, and Orthodox Jews. Moral Majority, Christian Voice USA, Christian Coalition of America, Eagle Forum, and The Family, a Christian political organization, Pat Robertson's Christian Coalition and Christian Broadcasting Network, Dr. James Dobson's group Focus on the Family, the Family Research Council, Robert Grant's Christian Voice, Jerry

Falwell's Moral Majority, Ed McAteer's Religious Roundtable Council, the Unification Church, The Family Research Council, the Liberty Counsel, The American Center for Law and Justice, and let's not forget funky Fred Phelps and the Westboro Baptist Church. There are many, many others.

There are a number of Universities that teach these wackadoo radical Religious Right Ideas, Bob Jones University, Oral Roberts University, Liberty University, Regent University, and Patrick Henry College.

Then there is the Media wing of the Christian Right, which include The 700 Club, the Christian Broadcasting Network, The Family Channel and our old friends at the Fox News Channel.

There are some Corporations that fall into this category as well, however that is a rant for another day.

Please do not confuse the concept of the Religious right as a demonizing of all churches or religion. I actually believe that they have the right to be political. My issue is that they are all in breach of IRS law and should pay their actual fair share of taxes. All donations and tithes should be taxed as ordinary income or all gross income above operating costs should be taxed at the corporate tax rate. What do you think about this?

Our Sort of Original Motto

"E Pluribus Unum" is used on all of our currency, and has been used on all of our currency since 1786. "In God we trust" first appeared on U.S. coins in 1864 and has appeared on paper currency since 1957. It was considered a de facto motto of the United States. Contrary to popular belief the motto "In God We Trust" was not the US motto until 1956. It had been lobbied for by Christians since the mid 1800s but not until the Communist/Atheist propaganda of the 1950s was it made into law.

"E Pluribus Unum," was proposed for the first Great Seal of the United States by John Adams, Benjamin Franklin and Thomas Jefferson in 1776, and also appears on all of our coins and some of our bills. The seal is used to authenticate certain documents issued by the United States federal government. The phrase is used both for the physical seal itself, and more generally for the design impressed upon it. The Great Seal was first used publicly in 1782. The obverse of the great seal is used as the national coat of arms of the United States. It is officially used on documents such as United States passports, military insignia, embassy placards, and various flags. Since 1935, both sides of the

Great Seal have appeared on the reverse of the one-dollar bill.

A far more inclusive motto "E Pluribus Unim" is more in line with the original secular vision of America and that is what should be on our currency. Conversely "In God we Trust" should not be used very specifically because it discriminates against non believers thereby alienating approximately 20% of Americans.

George HW Bush

George HW Bush for the most part was a pragmatist, he tried to reign in government spending with cuts but compromised and raised taxes as well.

What is of note is that the Bush family has a long history of support for Planned Parenthood. Prescott Bush, father of George HW Bush was the treasurer of Planned Parenthood when it launched it's first national fund raising campaign in 1947. Both George and First Lady Barbara were pro choice, however when Bush Sr. was asked to be Vice president on the Reagan ticket Reagan made him denounce his position.

George W Bush

I keep hearing Conservatives and Republicans say that I have to stop blaming President Bush for the problems we have Today. I will continue to blame Little Bush and the Republicans from now, until the day I die, or until the facts become NOT true.

No amount of repair by any President that followed George W Bush will be enough. The damage he did on America shall be taught to many, many generations of Americans in the future. History shall judge him for the buffoon that he was. George W Bush is the reason I will never, ever vote for any Republican ever again.

Here are some highlights from the disaster that was the Bush Administration.

He stole the presidency in 2000. People may forget that Republicans in Florida purged more than fifty thousand African American voters right before Election Day, and then he went to the Supreme Court where the GOP appointed majority stopped the recount that would have given the presidency to Al Gore if all of those votes were counted. National news organizations verified that fact long after Bush was sworn in.

Bush's lies started in that campaign. Bush ran for office claiming he was a "Uniter, not a divider." Even though he received fewer popular votes than Gore, he quickly claimed he had a mandate from the American people to push his right wing nut agenda.

He covered up his sordid past. He was a party boy, the spoiled son of a powerful political family who got away with desertion during the Vietnam War. He was reportedly AWOL for over a year from his assigned unit, the Texas Air National Guard, which other military outfit's called the "Champagne Division." He was known to be a heavy drinker and cocaine user.

He just loved the death penalty. As Texas governor from 1995 thru 2000, he signed more execution orders of any governor in US history, One hundred and fifty-two people, including the mentally ill, and women who were domestically abused. He spared just one man's life, a serial killer.

He was a loathsome corporate shill from day one. Bush got the GOP nomination by raising more campaign money from corporations than anyone up till then. He met with CEOs who would fly to Austin to "educate" him with their political wish lists.

He completely railed all US involvement in the global political scene. He forced the US out of the Kyoto Protocol, which laid out requirements for almost forty nations to lower greenhouse gasses and control climate change, saying that the agreement would "harm our economy and hurt our workers."

He embraced global isolationism in every aspect except trade. He withdrew from the 1972 Anti-Ballistic Missile Treaty, over Russia's protest, taking the US in an anti global direction not seen since the beginning of the last century.

Bush ignored warnings about Osama bin Laden. He ignored the Aug. 6, 2001 White House intelligence briefing titled, "Bin Laden determined to strike in the US" Meanwhile, his main anti-terrorism adviser, Richard Clarke, and first Treasury Secretary, Paul O'Neill, testified in Congress that he was intent on invading Iraq within days of becoming president.

Ramped up the war on drugs, not terrorists. The Bush administration had twice as many FBI agents assigned to the war on drugs than fighting terrorism before 9/11, and kept thousands in that role after the terror attacks.

"My Pet Goat." He kept reading a picture book to grade school children for seven minutes after his top aides told him that the World Trade Centers had been attacked on 9/11. Then Air Force One flew away from Washington DC, vanishing for hours after the attack.

After the 9/11 terrorist attacks, President Bush didn't call for sacrifice. He called for shopping. "Get down to Disney World in Florida," he said. "Take your families and enjoy life, the way we want it to be enjoyed." Taken on it's own, this wasn't such a horrible sentiment. But Boston University historian Andrew Bacevich has made a convincing case that it was part of a broader pattern of encouraging financial irresponsibility.

Squandered global goodwill after 9/11. Bush

thumbed his nose at world sympathy for the victims of the September 11, 2001 attacks, by declaring a global war on terrorism and declaring "You are either with us or against us."

Bush turned to Iraq not Afghanistan. The Bush administration soon started beating war drums for an attack on Iraq, where there was no proven Al Qaeda link, instead of Afghanistan, where the 9/11 bombers had trained and Osama bin Laden was based. His 2002 State of the Union speech declared that Iraq was part of an "Axis of Evil."

Attacked United Nation weapons inspectors. The march to war in Iraq started with White House attacks on the credibility of UN weapons inspectors in Iraq, whose claims that Saddam Hussein did not have nuclear weapons proved to be true.

He flat out lied about Iraq's weapons. In a major speech in October 2002, he said that Saddam Hussein had the capacity to send unmanned aircraft to the US with bombs that could range from chemical weapons to nuclear devices. "We cannot wait for the final proof, the smoking gun, that could come in the form of a mushroom cloud," his administration said.

He ignored the UN and launched a war. The Bush administration tried to get the UN Security

Council to authorize an attack on Iraq, which it refused to do. Bush then decided to lead a "preemptive" attack regardless of international consequences. He did not wait for any congressional authorization to launch a war.

Abandoned international Criminal Court. Before invading Iraq, Bush told the UN that the U.S. was withdrawing from ratifying the International Criminal Court Treaty to protect American troops from persecution and to allow it to pursue preemptive war.

Colin Powell's was convinced to give false evidence at the United Nations. The then Secretary of State gave a presentation based on lies. All the while the mainstream media started banging on the drums of war. All an effort of folly, a guise to start a war of choice on Saddam Hussein and Iraq.

Bush railed against CIA whistle blowers. Former ambassador Joe Wilson wrote a New York Times op-ed stating there was "No nuclear threat from Iraq". the White House retaliated by leaking his wife's name and destroying her career. Remember the Valerie Plame incident? She was at the time a CIA national security expert.

Bush pardoned the guy who did the leaking. Bush pardoned VP Cheney's top staffer, Scooter

Libby, for leaking Plame's name to the news.

Bush just had to have his Iraq War. In April 2003, the US military invaded Iraq again, leading to hundreds of thousands of civilian deaths and a million plus refugees. Nearly 6,700 U.S. soldiers died in the Iraq and Afghan wars.

Baghdad was looted systemically, every national treasure, vase and painting. All except for the oil ministry. Their was no plan for a military occupation or transition to civilian rule. A complete military fail. This war was started for oil, not terrorism. Just oil.

The war did not make the US safer. In 2006, a National Intelligence Estimate (a consensus report of the heads of 16 U.S. intelligence agencies) asserted that the Iraq war had increased Islamic radicalism and had worsened the terror threat.

US troops were given unsafe gear. From inadequate vests from protection against snipers to HumVees that could not protect soldiers from roadside bombs, the military did not sufficiently equip it's soldiers in Iraq, leading to an epidemic of brain injuries.

Meanwhile, the war propaganda continued. From landing on an aircraft carrier in a flight suit to declare "Mission Accomplished" to surprising troops in Baghdad with a Thanksgiving turkey that was a table decoration used as a prop, Bush defended his war of choice by using soldiers as PR props.

He never attended soldiers' funerals. For years after the war started, Bush never attended a funeral even though as of June 2005, 144 soldiers (of the 1,700 killed thus far) were laid to rest in Arlington National Cemetery, about two miles from the White House.

The Iraq war was Bush's single most destructive action, wasting $3 Trillion dollars in treasure and the killing of well over 100,000 souls, including 5000 US men and women serving in our armed services.

The Iraq war created the federal debt crisis. The total costs of the Iraq and Afghan wars will be somewhere between $4 trillion and $6 trillion, when the long-term veteran's medical costs are added in. Earlier reports were that the wars cost about $2 billion a week.

Meanwhile, war profiteering surged. The list of top Bush administration officials whose former corporate employers made billions in Pentagon contracts starts with Bush's VP Dick Cheney and Halliburton, which made almost $40 billion, and his daughter, Liz Cheney, who ran a $300 million Middle East partnership program.

Bush simply ignored the international ban on torture. Suspected terrorists were captured and tortured by the U.S. military in Baghdad's Abu Gharib prison, in the worst example of how the Bush White House ignored the Geneva Convention, that banned torture, and a secret prison system was born.

He Created the quagmire that is Guantanamo Bay, and began renditions. Rendition is where the US takes someone accused of being a terrorist somewhere out of the US and interrogates them using torture. The Bush White House created the military prison at Guantanamo Bay, Cuba. Many secret holding sites in Eastern Europe to go around both US domestic and military justice systems. Many of the men still jailed in Cuba were turned over to the US military by bounty hunters.

Bush raped the US Constitution as well. Bush made a mockery of basic civil liberties by launching a huge domestic spying program. Millions of Americans' online activities were monitored through telecommunications companies. The government, or the National Security Agency, the NSA had no search warrants or legal authority for it's electronic dragnet.

71

He cut veterans' healthcare funding. Right in the middle of the Iraq war, the White House cut funding for veterans' healthcare by billions of dollars, slashed a billion plus from military housing and fought extending healthcare to National Guard families, even as they were asked again and again for extended and repeat deployments.

Tax cuts for the rich. Bush decided to cut income taxes. In 2001 and 2003, he lowered income tax rates, cutting federal revenues as the cost of the foreign wars went up. The tax cuts benefited the wealthy, most going to the top one percent of incomes compared to 8.9% going to the middle 20 percent. The cuts were supposed to expire in 2013, but most are still in place. This tax cut was the biggest contributing factor to the deficit. In fact had Bush not signed these tax cuts the deficit would have been paid off by 2008.

Assault on reproductive rights. From his first term, the Bush administration led a serious fight on reproductive rights. He cut funds for UN family planning programs, barred military bases from offering and performing abortions, put right wing religious loonies in regulatory positions where they rejected new birth control drugs, and issued regulations making fetuses, but not women, eligible for federal healthcare.

Cut Pell Grant loans for students. His administration froze Pell Grants and tightened eligibility requirements for loans. This affected one and a half million poorer students. He eliminated federal job training programs that were intended to help young people.

Turned corporations loose on the environment. Bush's environmental record was incredibly bad, abandoning a campaign promise to tax carbon emissions and then pulling out of from the Kyoto accord. The Sierra Club lists 300 direct actions his staff took to end run around federal laws, cutting enforcement budgets, putting lobbyists in charge of agencies,making secret energy policies.

Bush Said "Evolution is a theory, just like intelligent design." One of his most inflammatory comments was saying that "Public schools should teach that evolution is a theory with as much validity as the religious belief in intelligent design, or God's active hand in creating life."

Lousy school reform. Bush's "No Child Left Behind" initiative made preparation for standardized tests and resulting test scores the top priority in schools. teachers felt that there was more to learning than taking tests. This program was not funded by the Federal government, and caused big money problems for most States.

Bush appointed a whole bunch of right-wing judges. Bush's two Supreme Court picks, Chief Justice John Roberts and Associate Justice Samuel Alito, have sided with pro-business on almost every issue. And talk about social conservatives, yikes! He also raised US District Court Judge Charles Pickering to an appeals court, despite his racist segregationist views.

Gutted the DOJ's voting rights section. Bush's Justice Department appointees led a multi year effort to prosecute so called voter fraud, including firing seven US attorneys who did not pursue overtly political cases because of lack of evidence.

Meanwhile average household incomes fell. When Bush took office in 2000, median household incomes were $52,500. In 2008, they were $50,303, a drop of 4.2 percent, making Bush the only recent two-term president to preside over such a drop.

And millions more fell below the poverty line. When Bill Clinton left office, 31.6 million Americans were living in poverty. When Bush left office, there were 39.8 million, according to the US Census, an increase of 26.1 percent. The Census said two-thirds of that growth occurred before the economic downturn of 2008.
Poverty among children also exploded. The

Census also found that 11.6 million children lived below the poverty line when Clinton left office. Under Bush, that number grew by 21 percent to 14.1 million.

Millions more lacked access to healthcare. Following these poverty trends, the number of Americans without health insurance was 38.4 million when Clinton left office. When Bush left, that figure had grown by nearly 8 million to 46.3 million, the Census found. Those with employer-provided benefit's fell every year he was in office.

Bush let black New Orleans drown. Hurricane Katrina exposed Bush's attitude toward the poor. Many said this reflected his views on blacks as well. He didn't visit the city after the storm destroyed the poorest sections. He praised his Federal Emergency Management Agency director for doing a "heck of a job" as the federal government did little to help thousands in the storm's aftermath and rebuilding.

Bush pandered to the religious right. Months before Katrina hit, Bush flew back to the White House to sign a bill to try to stop the comatose Terri Schiavo's feeding tube from being removed, saying the sanctity of life was at stake.

Set record for fewest press conferences. During his first term that was defined by the 9/11 attacks, he had the fewest press conferences of any modern president and had never met with the New York Times editorial board. But took the most vacation time. Reporters analyzing Bush's record found that he took off 1,020 days in two four-year terms, more than one out of every three days. No other modern president comes close. Bush also set the record for the longest vacation among modern presidents, five weeks, the Washington Post noted.

Karl Rove, Dick Cheney, Donald Rumsfeld. What a trio of power hungry, arrogant, ignorant buffoons. Not since the Watergate burglary and expansion of the Vietnam War have there been so many nitwit's in power. Cheney essentially ran the White House, Rove the political propaganda machine for corporations and the religious right, and Rumsfeld ran the wars to benefit the industrial military complex.

Bush eluded accountability for his actions. From Iraq war General Tommy Franks' declaration that "we don't do body counts" to numerous efforts to impeach Bush and top administration officials, primarily over launching the war in Iraq, he has never been held to account in any official domestic or international court or tribunal.

He basically stole the 2004 election. The closest Bush ever came to having to answer for his presidency was the 2004 election, which came down to the swing state of Ohio. Many believe that Karl Rove had somehow altered the Ohio results, the group "Anonymous" said that he did. GOP voter suppression tactics rivaled Florida in 2000 and many unresolved questions remain about whether the former GOP Secretary of State had Election Night totals altered in some counties.

His official policy of laissez faire by the SEC created an atmosphere that allowed unethical and criminal behavior rule wall street. Bank leverage was allowed to increase from 12% to 40%, derivatives were completely non regulated allowing unstable financial products to be created and sold world wide.

Limit's on Sub Prime Mortgages were allowed to expand from 4% to unlimited.

George Bush left the White House with a dismal economic record. By almost every measure; GDP growth, jobs, median incomes, financial-market performance. He stacks up as the least successful President on the economic front since Herbert Hoover.

When President Bush took office in 2001, Republicans and Democrats in Washington had built a strong consensus on the need for fiscal responsibility. Bush blew that apart within a few months. With the country in a recession, a temporary return to deficit's was inevitable. But Bush's tax cuts and spending increases, and clear disdain for the pay-as-you-go approach that had brought deficit's down in the 1990s

Energy policy, oh wait there was none, just Dick Cheney's secret meetings with the oil and gas companies and then having all gas drilling and hydraulic fracturing completely exempted from the Clean Air Act and The Clean Water Act. As far as I am concerned this is tantamount to treason. How dare they give away our natural resources and promote such an enormous amount of water and air pollution, not to mention the absolutely ginormous quantities of water required to be wasted on Hydraulic fracturing.

A side note to Bushes No Energy policy was that not a single step had been taken to cut our dependency on Foreign Oil.

Every Administration spins and sugarcoats the economic truth. But the Bush White House took this dis-ingenuousness to new levels. The surest way to get yourself fired as a Bush economic adviser was to say something that was true. Paul

O'Neill was ousted from Treasury for warning about deficit's. Larry Lindsey was kicked out of the top White House economic job for predicting in 2002 that the Iraq war would cost $100 billion to $200 billion, far below the actual cost but much more than what the White House was officially projecting. This disdain for reality, and for expertise, pervaded the Bush economic approach, and made it impossible for the Administration to react intelligently to real world problems like the housing bubble.

TARP was the brainchild of Hank Paulson, Bushes Treasury Secretary at the time. Something had to be done, and by golly they done did it, unfortunately by time they put Elizabeth Warren in charge of overseeing the counting of the dollars the whole first half of the TARP money had been given out and nobody knew where it went. My guess is that most of it was stolen, literally tens of billions of dollars went missing, and nobody knew where. Just another example of incompetence and fiscal mismanagement.

The Legacy of the George W Bush Presidency is as follows;

An absolute mountain of debt in the form of huge deficit's. Nearly almost complete economic system collapse. The epic recession, second only to the Great Depression in our history. Record Budget deficit's. Unbelievable, unprecedented job loss. Complete income stagnation. Chaos and Corruption. Destruction of wealth and retirement. Dismantling of health care in the US. Giant income shift away from the working middle classes and the poor to the very wealthy. Not one, but two completely unnecessary wars that depleted our treasure and killed thousands of young American soldiers. Bush was a failure by every know metric. The damage caused by his policies and decisions will leave America crippled for decades.

Happy Birthday Mr. Bush. I hope you choke on your cake.

Here is a list of George W Bush "Benghazi" type attacks that nobody said a word about.

September 11, 2001 - Might as well mention that the attack on the twin towers on 9/11 was on Bush's watch.

January 22, 2002. Calcutta, India. Gunmen associated with Harkat-ul-Jihad al-Islami attack the U.S. Consulate. Five people are killed.

June 14, 2002. Karachi, Pakistan. Suicide bomber connected with al Qaeda attacks the U.S. Consulate, killing 12 and injuring 51.

October 12, 2002. Denpasar, Indonesia. U.S. diplomatic offices bombed as part of a string of "Bali Bombings." No fatalities.

February 28, 2003. Islamabad, Pakistan. Several gunmen fire upon the U.S. Embassy. Two people are killed.

May 12, 2003. Riyadh, Saudi Arabia. Armed al Qaeda terrorists storm the diplomatic compound, killing 36 people including nine Americans. The assailants committed suicide by detonating a truck bomb.

July 30, 2004. Tashkent, Uzbekistan. A suicide bomber from the Islamic Movement of Uzbekistan attacks the U.S. Embassy, killing two people.

December 6, 2004. Jeddah, Saudi Arabia. Al Qaeda terrorists storm the U.S. Consulate and occupy the perimeter wall. Nine people are killed.

March 2, 2006. Karachi, Pakistan again. Suicide bomber attacks the U.S. Consulate killing four people, including U.S. diplomat David Foy who was directly targeted by the attackers. (I wonder if Lindsey Graham or Fox News would even recognize the name "David Foy." This is the third Karachi terrorist attack in four years on what's considered American soil.)

September 12, 2006. Damascus, Syria. Four armed gunmen shouting "Allahu akbar" storm the U.S. Embassy using grenades, automatic weapons, a car bomb and a truck bomb. Four people are killed, 13 are wounded.

January 12, 2007. Athens, Greece. Members of a Greek terrorist group called the Revolutionary Struggle fire a rocket-propelled grenade at the U.S. Embassy. No fatalities.

March 18, 2008. Sana'a, Yemen. Members of the al-Qaeda-linked Islamic Jihad of Yemen fire a mortar at the U.S. Embassy. The shot misses the embassy, but hit's nearby school killing two.

July 9, 2008. Istanbul, Turkey. Four armed terrorists attack the U.S. Consulate. Six people are killed.

September 17, 2008. Sana'a, Yemen. Terrorists dressed as military officials attack the U.S. Embassy with an arsenal of weapons including RPGs and detonate two car bombs. Sixteen people are killed, including an American student and her husband (they had been married for three weeks when the attack occurred). This is the second attack on this embassy in seven months.

Here is a list of scandals associated with President GW Bush;

Abu-Gate is the term occasionally found identifying the acts of brutality, abuse, and torture at Abu Ghraib Enemy Prisoner of War camp in Iraq.

Compassiongate is the term used by the Compassiongate web site in trying to explain the Compassionate Conservatism, example; the Compassionate Conservatism of the Bush administration: "the dearth (but not lack) of a conscience."

CondiGate is the term used to describe Secretary of State Condoleezza Rice's (1) testimony given April 8, 2004, before the 9/11 Commission, and (2) "reported directive to her staff to keep mum" on John R. Bolton's nomination as ambassador to the United Nations in April 2005.

Foleygate is the term used in reference to the sex scandal revealed in late September 2006 involving former Republican Rep. Mark Foley's "simply naughty" e-mails sent to male teen pages. Until his September 29, 2006, immediate resignation

Gannongate is the term being applied to fake

news reporter James Guckert, alias "Jeff Gannon," who worked for fake news agency Talon News, with "daily passes" somehow obtained from the Secret Service and FBI which allowed Guckert/Gannon access to White House press briefings and to parse questions to President Bush.

Hookergate is the term given to the Congressional Bribery and a DC Sex Scandal.
Intimigate is the term coined by David Sirota of the Center for American Progress to describe "the well established pattern... That the Bush Administration has summarily fired, intimidated and defamed anyone who has had the courage to tell the truth about Iraq."

Memogate is the term used to describe allegations of Republican operatives hacking into the computer systems of Democratic members of Congress.

Rathergate: Sumner M. Redstone, George W. Bush & CBS

Rovegate and Treasongate both refer to Karl Rove's outing of Valerie Plame as a covert CIA operative. Also called "The Plame Game"

Scoregate is the term used regarding the "controversy over Medicare scoring... Richard

Foster, Medicare's top actuary, recently made headlines by suggesting that the White House may have been involved in keeping his estimates of the new Medicare law under wraps." It is also known as Medigate.

SnoopGate, so-named December 19, 2005, by Jonathan Alter, regarding George W. Bush's domestic spying.

UNscam is the name given to the scandal surrounding the United Nations' Oil for Food Program.

Halliburton's Corruption

CIA Pre 9/11 Intelligence Failures The massive intelligence failure that led Bush to lie to the world about the Iraqi threat is under investigation by a congressional authorized independent commission, which Bush fought the creation of.

Suppressed Medicare costs (HHS) and bio-terrorism studies (DOD)

Bush's Medicare scam and the circumstances that led the administration to lie to Congress about the cost of the legislation is under investigation by the HHS inspector general's office. Bribes offered on the House floor to Rep. Nick Smith (R-MI) in exchange for his vote on

Bush's Medicare plan are under investigation by the House Ethics Committee and the Justice Department.

HHS Deceptive Ad Campaign

HHS Scully Scandal

Government-wide Accounting Problems

Sex Education Misinformation

CAPPS II Failures

Real Costs of the Iraq War

Iraq, the reason for, cost of, and occupation of, following America's crusade (DOS, DOD, CIA, FBI).

Lacking terrorism readiness and prevention, both domesticity and international, before and after 9/11 (CIA, FBI, DOD, etc.);

Increasing fiscal deficit's and tax relief only for the wealthy (Treasury, OMB).

Skewed and suppressed scientific data, research and policies. (NASA, NIH, HHS, FDA, EPA).

Dick Cheney's secret "Energy Task Force" was

investigated by the GAO and the case is currently still pending at the Supreme Court.

The Homeland and Lilly Protection Act.

Attorney General John Ashcroft was under investigation by the Federal Election Commission for violating campaign finance laws in 2000, and the FEC concluded that Ashcroft accepted $110,000 in illegal contributions.

An investigation into House Majority Leader Tom DeLay's criminal fund-raising schemes in Texas. which used corporate funds to help state GOP lawmakers is already before a Texas grand jury Republican staffers on the Senate Judiciary Committee were investigated for stealing thousands of confidential memos from Dem computers, a matter that has now been referred to the Justice Department for a possible criminal probe.

Republican Connecticut Gov. John Rowland is under a criminal investigation (and an impeachment investigation) after he lied about prominent state contractors and several government aides paying for refurbishments to his lake-front cottage.

Former Rep. Bill Janklow (R-S.D.) was under investigation for vehicular manslaughter, a crime for which he was later convicted.

The Pentagon launched a formal investigation into well-armed evangelist and three-star General William G. Boykin, Bush's pick for deputy undersecretary of defense for intelligence, and his record of extreme religious rhetoric.

And honorable mentions should go, of course, to investigations into Enron who was in fact George W Bush's biggest corporate supporter.

Recently we have seen news reports of the NSA gathering all of our phone call data as well as all of our email and online activity data. Somehow people are shocked and surprised. This is old news folks. Your Fourth Amendment Rights were stripped clean. As if the whole amendment were just ripped out of the Constitution. It is important to understand who did this to you.

The Fourth Amendment of the United States Constitution is part of the Bill of Rights which outlaws "unreasonable searches and seizures." Requires all warrants to be supported by probable cause. It was adopted as a response to the abuses of the "writ of assistance", which was a type of general search warrant used during the Revolutionary war. Search, seizure, and arrest should be limited in scope. The Fourth

Amendment applies to individual states by the "Due Process Clause of the Fourteenth Amendment."

The "Patriot Act of 2001" was passed by Congress and signed into law by George W Bush on October 26, 2001.

Passed right after, and because of, the 9/11 terrorist attack, it lifted many, many restrictions on all law enforcement, very much so with regard to gathering of intelligence. Expanded the Treasury Secretary's power over all financial transactions, especially those of foreign persons and companies. Broadened law enforcement overall as well, Immigration so they can more easily detain and deport anyone suspected of terrorism. The act also expanded the actual definition of terrorism to include the domestic kind, so that the administration can accuse anyone of being a terrorist, and so expanding activities of when the Patriot Act's powers can be used.

On May 26, 2011, President Barack Obama signed the Patriot Sunsets Extension Act of 2011, a four year extension of three key parts in the US Patriot Act. Roving wiretaps, searches of business records and conducting surveillance of "lone wolves" or individuals suspected of terrorist related activities not linked to terrorist groups.

Using the panic created by the 9/11 attack and the 2001 anthrax care, Congress rushed to pass legislation to strengthen National security. Taking full advantage of the fear mongering. Democrats mostly disagreed.

Opponents argue against the indefinite detention clause, this is what allowed Guantanamo Bay Prison. Law enforcement can now legally search a home or business without permission. Expanded use allows the FBI to search phone, email, and financial records, business records, without a warrant or court order. Many law suit's have been brought against it, and Federal courts have ruled that some provisions are unconstitutional.

Many of the act's parts were to automatically go away beginning December 31, 2005, about four years after it was passed. Before that date, supporters pushed to make it's provisions permanent, critics tried to revise parts to better protect civil liberties. In 2005, the Senate passed a re-authorization bill with changes to many sections, while the House re-authorization bill kept most of the original wording intact. The two bills were reconciled and was criticized by both parties for ignoring civil liberties. The bill, which removed most of the changes from the Senate version, passed in March 2006, and was signed into law by President George W Bush.

The NSA warrant less surveillance controversy or "Warrant less Wiretapping" concerns surveillance of persons within the United States during the collection of foreign intelligence by the U.S. National Security Agency NSA as part of the war on terror. Under this program, referred to by the Bush administration as the "terrorist surveillance program," part of the broader President's Surveillance Program, the NSA was authorized by executive order to monitor, without search warrants, the phone calls, Internet activity, text messaging, Web, e-mail, etc... Other communication involving any party believed by the NSA to be outside the US, even if the other end of the communication lies within the US Critics, however, claimed that it was in an effort to attempt to silence critics of the Bush Administration and their handling of several hot button issues during it's tenure. Under public pressure, the Bush administration ceased the warrant less wiretapping program in January 2007 and returned review of surveillance to the FISA court. The FISA court is a fancy way to say "Under the Patriot Act".

So now you know exactly how the Conservatives and Republicans took away your Forth Amendment Rights. Don't any of you even think about spinning this as a President Obama Scandal. Bush and Cheney are the criminals here, they are the ones who should have been impeached and imprisoned. This was one of the main reasons I am no longer a Republican and will never vote for a Republican again. Although, I am really pissed at Obama for extending most of it for an additional four years. He should have known, and done better.

Corporate Fascism

Who are the REAL Moochers and Takers in America?

$100 Billion or $870 per family for Federal Direct Subsidies and Grants to Companies in Farm, high-tech R&D, overseas promotion of US products and industries.

$80 Billion or $696 per family for Business Incentives at the State, County and City Levels

$83 Billion or $722 per family for Interest Rate Subsidies for Banks. These are subsidies paid directly to JP Morgan, Bank of America, Citigroup, Wells Fargo, Goldman Sachs, etc...

$40 Billion or $350 per family for Retirement Fund Bank Fees. Taken directly from taxpayers accounts.

$145 Billion or $1,268 per family for Overpriced Medications. Government granted patent monopolies to the drug companies cause this price gauging.

$184 Billion or $1600 per family for Corporate Tax Subsidies. This is the tax breaks for the super rich.

$141 Billion or over $1,200 per family for Revenue Loss from Corporate "Tax Havens"or loopholes. The wealthy and the corporations hide their money in offshore accounts and just refuse to pay US taxes on this money.

Total $774 Billion or $6,700 per family is being paid to subsidize corporations that have doubled their profit's and cut their taxes in half over the last 10 years, all while off shoring 3 Million US jobs.

These facts used above were inspired from an article published on Bill Moyers website written by Paul Buchheit and quoted the following sources: Cato Institute, The New York Times, The Huffington Post, Demos, Economic Policy Institute, Dean Baker, OECD, Citizens for Tax Justice, Government accountability Office, and US PIRG. To clarify further the amounts are based on family income of $75k per year, and I checked the math on the basis of 115 million families that this applied too. I admit there is a margin of error within the numbers certainly. However I believe that it represents a reasonable truth.

Privatization of Governmental services has been by and large a monumental failure as a policy. While a push to privatize just about everything over the last 30 years has met with perceived success the truth is far from.

Privatized military contracts to supply food and materials to our troops in the field, the building of facilities, and security details using private soldiers. The results are excessive food pricing to military personnel, for instance one contractor charges $14 for a 6 pack of Coca-Cola. Facility contractors have used unqualified employees to build in theater KBR built shower stalls that electrocuted soldiers because they used local "electricians" that were not qualified. Just the mention of the Blackwater company invokes mass shootings of civilians during security runs. Costs have gone up exponentially and no bid contracts are the norm.

Privatization increases bureaucracy and cost because if the Government does something the goal is service not profit. In the Roman Republic private individuals and companies performed the majority of services including tax collection (tax farming), army supplies (military contractors), religious sacrifices and construction. Many scholars suggest that the cost of bureaucracy was one of the reasons for the fall of the Roman Empire.

Comprehensive social welfare analysis of the British privatization program had surprisingly small effects on firms and most employees, and generally harmed taxpayers and most consumers.

Privatizations in Russia and Latin America were increased corruption, people with political connections unfairly amassed huge wealth. This discredited privatization in these regions. Privatization in Latin America has lately experienced increasing push back from the public.

Natural Monopoly - The most efficient number of firms in some industries, such as tap water is one. Therefore it is better to have a public monopoly rather than a private monopoly which can exploit the consumer.

Public Interest - Public services should not be for profit. For example, in the case of health care, privatized health care means a greater priority is given to profit than patient care.

Public borrowing will continue to increase because the government no longer gets the profit's.

Problem is you can not regulate private monopolies, and private monopolies are illegal.

Rail Privatization in the UK was unsuccessful

The latest privatization fail is the background check company USIS which does just under half of all US Government and Military security checks. They did the background checks for Edward Snowden and the Navy Yard shooter Aaron Alexis. Apparently they get paid by the quantity not quality of work done. Now it has come to light that tens of thousands of security checks may have been done poorly.

What have we saved? Has privatization helped or hurt us? The answers are clear. Privatization as a concept may sound good, but in practical application is a complete fail.

Here is a partial List of Corporations that pay zero in taxes;
Verizon
MetLife
Eaton
Regeneron Pharmaceuticals
Public Storage
Ventas
Avalonbay Communities
Agilent Technologies
Vornado Realty Trust
Boston Properites
Seagate Technology
Broadcom
News Corp
Lam Research
Kimco Realty
Waters

Macerich
Plum Creek Timber
PulteGroup
Apartment Investment & Management
Perkin Elmer

Taft-Hartley Act

To be more precise the Labor Management Relations act of 1947 better known as the Taft–Hartley Act, restricts the activities and power of labor unions. Originally vetoed by then President Truman, passed into law by congressional override. President Truman argued that it was a "dangerous intrusion on free speech," and that it would "conflict with important principles of our democratic society." labor leaders called it the "slave labor bill"

The bill was a deliberate effort on the part of Republicans to decrease the gains made by the labor movement, it put limit's on a unions right to strike.

Citizens United vs FEC

The First Amendment to the US Constitution prohibits the "making of any law abridging the freedom of speech". "Freedom of Speech" Does that apply to "Paid Speech"? Does paid speech equal free speech? I submit that if one has to pay actual money for speech, then it is no longer free. If all political speech will be considered paid speech from now on, then it would make sense that those who have the money to pay for it shall be heard and those with no money shall not be heard. Thereby "abridging" or reducing free speech for the common man.

The Citizens United vs Federal Election Commission Supreme Court ruling when taken at face value seems intended to protect speech though advertising. However when looked at through the lens of those who do not have the means to advertise, most certainly abridges the ability of average Americans to compete with Corporate monies.

The Citizens United ruling is unconstitutional on that basis. The Justice's got it wrong, or did they? Perhaps their intent was political, and not constitutional? Either way, altruistic, ideological, or corrupt. If a majority of us are against it, it should go. Multiple current polls suggest that more than 90% of Americans are against it.

Mission

Go directly to the source and take away their damn money.

Step 1 fight like heck to overturn Citizens United v FEC and the ruling that Corporations are people.

Step 2 get legislation passed to get all moneys out of politics.

Step 3 defund the lobbyists by making corporate money illegal to use to lobby.

Step 4 Make illegal all "Pacs" and "Super Pacs", also eliminate all tax exempt groups like the 501c except for 100% humanitarian and public health and safety groups. Any politics at all should immediately disqualify them.

Step 5 Go after all of those "activist" churches and religions with a vengeance. Remove their tax exempt status and their ability to give money to political causes.

While this is only the spearhead of a much broader mission, money is the root problem. Take away their money and you eliminate their ability to indoctrinate and brainwash. Anything else you may try to do will meet with absolute failure if the fuel to the motor is not stopped first.

104

Types of Republicans

Modified from the original article "The 7 Types Of Republicans And How To Debate Them"
By Matthew Desmond

If you've ever spent time trying to discuss politics with a Republican you've probably noticed that there are several different types of Republicans, all with their own unique debating style. In this article I'm going to attempt to break down the seven types of Republicans, what's wrong with their views, and how you should debate them. I'll start with the most intelligent, and work my way down.

The Educated Republicans - These are the rarest of all Republicans. Occasionally you will run into one in public or in a public forum online. These Republicans can be the most difficult to deal with. They have learned everything there is to know about their position from a Republican perspective. They've educated themselves on all the reasons why their position is correct, and are not concerned with anything that contradicts their beliefs. The problem with this type of Republican's views is that anyone with the Internet and five minutes can find something that thoroughly discredit's their version of the "facts." Even when confronted with contradictory facts, they continue to fall back on their original arguments; try to change the subject to something they are more comfortable talking about, or start expressing opinions with no factual merit.

What to remember when debating them, keep them on topic. Don't let them ignore your counterpoints and then change the subject on you. They're masters of that, but if you can keep them on topic, eventually they will just start expressing opinions to which you can say "do you have any facts to back that up?"

Fox News and Conservative Talk Radio Republicans - This is one of the angriest groups of Republicans. They watch Fox News or listen to conservative talk radio and they think it makes them an expert on politics. The only knowledge they have of politics are parroted talking points, without any facts to back them up. When you defeat them in debate, they will resort to calling you names like "liberal," "commie," "socialist"; "baby killer," etc. They think all liberals are socialists who want to take their money and give it to people who don't deserve it.

The problem with this type of Republican's views is that they have no idea what they are talking about. Usually they're just repeating things they've heard from Fox News or Rush Limbaugh. They think that liberals want to take away their freedoms and they clearly don't know what the word "liberal" means, or what liberals have contributed to our country and our freedoms. They think President Obama is comparable to Hitler for passing healthcare reform. They accuse you of watching MSNBC if you don't agree with them. They call you a sheep but expect you to blindly believe everything they tell you, without question.

What to remember when debating them is to keep demanding facts from them to back up their assertions until they break down and call you any of the aforementioned names. Ask them to name specific freedoms that liberals have taken away from them. They have a tendency to become violent so watch their hands if you are debating them face to face.

Christian Republicans - These Republicans are hypocrites. They do everything in the name of Christ, while simultaneously acting as un-Christ like as humanly possible. They support the right to carry assault weapons, are pro-war, and completely ignore the fact that the Bible depicts Christ as a liberal who was opposed to capitalism and violence. They sincerely believe that this is God's country and that God loves us Americans more than anyone else in the world. They think that anyone who is not 100 percent pro-Israel is anti-Semitic. They hate everyone who doesn't agree with them and think the Bible tells them to... and they hate gay people because they think they are sinners.

The problem with this type of Republican's views is that they do terrible things in the name of their Lord. They think that anyone who doesn't agree with them is damned to hell or hates America. They believe that we are a Christian nation even though the Founding Fathers made sure they did not brand this country as a Christian nation. The Founding Fathers wanted a country of religious freedom, free from religious persecution, but these Republicans will never admit that.

What to remember when debating them is that There is a list of all the quotes that prove our Founding Fathers wanted a country of religious freedom. Another thing to remember is that the Christian Right is neither. Start asking them questions like "how would Jesus feel about war?" "how would Jesus feel about assault rifles?" or "do you really think that America is God's favorite country, in the entire universe?" And, of course, these questions should yield a response that thoroughly proves that they are hypocrites, and continuing to argue with them would be a waste of time.

Tea Party Republicans - These Republicans are a dumbed down combination of the previous two groups of Republicans. They think Sarah Palin is intelligent and it's the media filter's fault that she looks so stupid. They think Reagan was fiscally conservative even though he tripled the deficit. They watch Fox News religiously, and think

Glenn Beck is credible. They don't understand why people think they're racist while they're standing next to people holding racist signs. They protest higher taxes even though taxes have gone down for 95 percent of working families since President Obama took office.

The problem with this type of Republican's views is that they parrot Glenn Beck and Sarah Palin talking points. When you discredit one thing they say, they immediately move on to the next subject. Anyone who doesn't agree with them is a socialist, even though they can't give you the actual definition of socialism. Many of them are on Medicare while protesting socialism. They have never met a socialist, so they have no idea what socialists believe. They think liberals are socialists and socialists are Nazis.

What to remember when debating them is that they have no idea what they're talking about. Ask them to prove what they are saying. If you ask them a question and they respond with another question, refuse to answer their question until they answer yours. Don't back down. Remind them that taxes have actually been lowered for 95 percent of working families. If debating them in public, be careful because they are known to carry guns in places they don't need them, like public parks and bars and churches.

Birther Republicans - the birthers think that Obama was born in Kenya. No matter how much evidence you present that is contradictory to that thesis, they will continue to insist that he is not the legitimate president. They are sore losers because McCain lost the election in 2008 even though President Obama has won reelection since then. They will never support Obama, even if he paid off the entire national debt.

The problem with this type of Republican's views is that they think Obama was born in Kenya. They think that Orly Taitz, who grew up in a communist country, is credible, and that Obama is a socialist. They think Donald Trump is a smart guy. They think that Obama's birth announcements in Hawaiian newspapers were propagated over 40 years in advance of his election, just so that he could be elected someday.

What to remember when debating them is don't waste your time. You could wave Obama's actual birth certificate in their face and they would still say it's a fake. They are sore-losers and they will never be happy as long as Obama is president. Make jokes asking to see their birth certificates, or Sarah Palin's birth certificate. This is the best way to get them to go away.

Racist Republicans - I am putting this one almost last for a reason. I do not think all Republicans are racists. I have Republican family members who are not racist. This section is only about the percentage of Republicans who are actually racist, because they do exist. I'm not "playing the race card" or "race-baiting," I'm just describing racists who affiliate themselves with the Republican Party

Racist Republicans hate Obama because he's black. They think that all Muslims are terrorists. They think Obama is a terrorist Muslim. They think anyone with a name like Obama's is a terrorist.

The problem with this type of Republican's views is that they're racist, but they think Obama is a racist. They can't understand why people call them racists when they post racist pictures or racist comments and then claim not to be racist. Whenever they possibly can, they will call you a racist, to hide the fact that they are actually racists.

What to remember when debating them is that they're racists. Racists are uneducated bigots. You would have a much easier time convincing an apple tree to start growing oranges.

Extremely Uneducated Republicans - these Republicans are Republicans because they think it's cool. They have a Republican friend in one of the other groups listed, so they think they know what they're talking about. They have terrible spelling and grammar but they expect you to believe whatever they say because they are saying it to you.

The problem with this type of Republican's views

is that it's hard to tell if they ever made it past the 4th grade. Most of their posts are illegible. They don't know anything about their position other than what they have heard their friends say. They think Republicans are fiscally conservative because they say that they are, and call anyone who doesn't agree with them "sheep." They ignore all historical information that is contradictory to what they say. They are 100 percent blind to facts.

What to remember when debating them is that no amount of facts or logic will ever convince them that their buddies are wrong. You could be a college professor and they will still think your facts aren't credible. Instead of trying to argue with them, try explaining algebra to your dog. I'm sure it will be much more productive.

Hopefully this has been an informative resource for you. I hope you will remember some of the things I have said the next time you are engaged in a debate with a Republican. There's definitely an overlap between several of these types, so you may have to utilize several different tactics to debate them.

A note for the last one, actually being a college professor, or even a college graduate, is actually a mark against you for convincing most of these. Many Republicans believe college and education are inherently suspect.

I would also add the people who were raised brain-washed by their parents.

One more thing, under the Christian Republican description, "They think that anyone who is not 100 percent pro-Israel is anti-Semitic." I would add a clause to that sentence: "yet they despise most Jews."

Even if Obama was born in Kenya he would still be the President legally because he was born a US citizen. Since his mother was a citizen and neither her identity as his mother nor her citizenship as an American was never called into question, Obama is a citizen, even if he was born on the moons of Mars he would be born an American citizen and therefore our legally elected president.

the "Manly Republican." These are Republicans because they think it makes them seem tougher and a "real man" because they are pro-gun, pro-war, anti homosexual, and think being a liberal and things like wanting to help the poor, save the environment, equal marriage rights makes you a pussy.

My discovery when debating with educated Republicans is that when you point out things that disprove their theories, they just repeat the theories louder, as if it will make them true by beating you with the same argument over and over, using their words as a club. It doesn't make it more true, except to themselves. The more they repeat the same old lame arguments, they succeed in only convincing themselves.

And they all have one thing in common: complete utter hatred of reality.

The Current Republican Agenda

What the hell is wrong with you Republicans and Conservatives?

Another mass shooting and you want video game control and blame single mothers? What are you people smoking? Geez.

Another debt ceiling limit and your gonna shut down the whole government if you don't get everything that you want? Are you 6? If you take your ball and go home nobody will vote for you again, Ever.

45% of you in Louisiana blame Obama for the mess after hurricane Katrina? Why not just blame him for sinking the Titanic as well? Crazy town!

Bringing up a 42nd vote to repeal Obamacare? Not too swift are you?

Iowa R & C says it's OK for blind people to carry guns? Wait, what?

North Carolina OK'ed gun permit's for crazy people. Maybe, we should take away their guns.

Texas pushing legislation to teach creationism in public school? WTF?

There is nothing conservative about any of this...

For all of you that say USA is "Number One" here is the truth.

Current US Ranking per category

Education - 13
Literacy - 7
Math - 27
Science – 22

Healthcare – 38
Infant Mortality rate - 178
Life expectancy - 50
Hepatitis B Vaccinations - 89
Infant Survival Rate – 47
Happiest - 11
Perceived Honesty - 24
Best place to be a mother 25 (Save The Children)
Women holding public office 79

Economic Mobility - 8
Median Household income - 3
Unemployment Percentage - 102
Minimum Wages – 13
Income inequality – 39
Starting A Business – 13
Economic Freedom - 10
Freedom of the Press - 47
Freedom from corruption - 22
GDP Growth - 169
GDP per Capita 12
Debt relative to GDP – 192

Debt insolvency – 15
Exports – 4
International Trade - 20
Industrial Production Growth Rate - 79
Infrastructure Investment -142
Net Trade of Goods and Services - 192 (Last)
Reserve of Foreign Exchange and Physical Gold
Holdings - 19

So what are we actually "Number One" in?

Highest incarceration rate in the world
Largest total prison population
Highest percentage of obese people
Highest divorce rate (by a wide margin)
Most hours of TV watched per person
Most total crimes
Highest rate of illegal drug use
Most car thefts (by far)
Most rapes
Most murders
Most police officers
The US spends more on health care as a % of
GDP than any other nation
More people on pharmaceutical drugs than any
other country
Most women taking antidepressants
Most student loan debt
Most pornography
Largest trade deficit Between 2000 - 2010, the
US had a total trade deficit of $6.1 trillion dollars
with the rest of the world, the US has had a

negative trade balance every year since 1976
Military Spending   U.S. military spending is greater than the military spending of China, Russia, Japan, India, and the rest of NATO combined.
Most foreign military bases
Most complicated tax system in the entire world.
The US has accumulated the biggest national debt in history
Selfish Rich People
Bigots, Racists, And Misogynists
Child like "Libertarians"
Rugged Individualists
Lunatic Fringe Conspiracy Theorists
Anti Science Christian Extremists
Fearful, Ignorant, Uneducated people

Here is a list of things Conservatives and Republicans believe is true or actually are in favor of, bills have been introduced on some issues. All of which are complete and utter nonsense, or as I like to call it "Pretzel Logic";

Climate change is a hoax.

Guns have nothing to do with gun violence.

Our nation is founded, and based, on Christianity, even though the word appears no where in our Constitution.

Rape victims who become pregnant should see it

as a blessing from God. This is a lot more common than you'd think.

Homosexuals threaten heterosexual relationships, and our society

The best way to worship Jesus Christ is by hating, judging and fearing anyone who's different

Equal rights, and pay, for women are debatable

Woman's health, and control of their bodies, is best decided by a group of men

Strongly detest abortions, yet: Oppose sex education and access to free contraceptives for the poor

Claim to be pro-life, yet: Support the death penalty, then brag about the frequency for which it is used

Claim they love our Constitution, then openly state they will defy any Constitutionally upheld laws of which they disagree

Talk about individual freedoms being at risk, then openly support bans on same-sex marriage

Say they love our country, and are true patriots, then scream secession anytime they don't get their way

That sexual orientation is a choice, but can't identify when they chose to be straight

They're fiscally responsible, yet haven't voted for a Republican President who didn't drastically grow our national debt
Government doesn't create jobs, yet millions are employed by the government

The best way for the poor and middle class to become rich, is by giving rich people more money

You can't credit Obama with the death of Bin Ladin, because he didn't personally pull the trigger (or he was already dead)

The science of evolution is on equal standing as Creationism

Improving our education system is best served by paying teachers less, calling them lazy and cutting funding for educational programs

4 Americans dying in Benghazi is more appalling than the over 4,000 who died in Iraq
President Obama isn't really an American, a good 25-30% of Republicans are still "birthers".

Fox News is "fair and balanced" and the "lamestream media" is just a puppet for liberal propaganda, then brags about Fox News being Americans most watched cable news channel, the definition of mainstream media (though their ratings are plummeting)

What A Nation Might Look Like Built on Republican Ideology
By Allen Clifton

Republicans believe that their ideology is what the United States needs in order to be "successful and prosperous." Which always forces me to ask the question, "If conservative ideology is so wonderful, why are so many of their states poor, rank near the bottom in median family income and their citizens have shorter life expectancy than people living in "liberal states?" Of course it's a rhetorical question because most conservatives either won't answer the question or simply deny that it's true. It's a question which challenges their cognitive dissonance, which means for many they simply can't grasp the conflicting realities of what they want to believe and what's actually there. But it did get me to thinking, what kind of country do these people want? What might it be like? What would their social structures be like? So, I decided I'd try to paint a picture of what kind of nation these people want. Based upon what I've seen many Republicans support, if they had their way, they would have a country that:
Had a government based upon theocracy where all but one religion is vilified.

Women are seen as secondary citizens to men, and their rights would often be determined by only men.

Rape victims would often be viewed as poorly as those who committed the crime.

Prayer would be required in schools.

Homosexuality would be seen as an abomination.

Contraceptives would be strongly frowned upon or would be outright illegal.

Voting laws, and rules, would be structured to favor a particular section of it's citizens.

Having an abortion would be an offense equal to murder (and punished as such).

Immigrants wouldn't be welcome.

Anyone who opposed Republican beliefs would be viewed as an enemy to God and country.

Nationalism would be used as a tool to breed intolerance of anyone different.

Same-sex marriage wouldn't be legal.

Homosexuals wouldn't be allowed to adopt children. Education would be manipulated by the theocratic beliefs of the government.

Wait, this all sounds very familiar. I know I've heard of a country that shares many of these same values... Oh that's right, Iran

Republicans are Doomed

The Republican Party's voter base is continually shrinking. While Republicans hold a majority in the House thanks to "Gerrymandering", the Senate is not held by the GOP and neither is the White House. In fact, no Republican candidate has easily won the White House since 1988 when George HW Bush beat Michael Dukakis in a landslide. The largest GOP demographic is the over 65 crowd, and in particular older white Americans.

Over the last four election cycles the GOP has lost approximately 3% of their base per cycle. Some of that shrinkage is people getting so old and sick that they do not go out and vote any longer. Part of that group has passed away. Another chunk of people have stopped identifying with them and have changed from calling themselves Republican and now consider themselves Independents, Libertarians, or even, gulp, Democrats.

Polls from just a year or so ago showed a solid 35%-40% lead in this Base demographic, but recent polling shows that GOP threats to potentially cut Social Security, Medicare, and Medicaid have dropped that huge lead into the far less secure 2%-4% area. The GOP has overestimated their loyalty vs their safety and security.

The Republican Party is becoming even more extreme right wing. More extreme, period. It wasn't acceptable to openly accuse the President of treason and call for impeachment for imaginary crimes a decade ago. At least not according to in the rank and file of the party.

Yes, I know that Bill Clinton lied under oath about Monica Lewinsky, but that was an actual case of proven perjury and not the delusions of some far right nuts who believe President Obama went back in time and forged his own birth certificate. Rather than evolving on issues and moving back to the 'Big Tent" ideology of being ever more inclusive, they have moved the pendulum further and extremely further to the Right. They have no intention of expanding their Party to include those which they despise, no, they will take a road much different. Their policies are to Gerrymander whatever districts and or States that they can to impose an apartheid hold on their seats. Use voter suppression against every demographic   presented here. Force law changes through the legislative process at all levels and use the Justice system to gut existing law. Clearly redistricting, or Gerrymandering, voter ID laws, restrictions of early voting rules, limiting of voting machines, and the return of Jim Crow laws in the South like Poll Taxes, literacy tests, or outright intimidation shall be the norm.

The SCOTUS Citizens United ruling has allowed corporate and special interest money to flow to their benefit. They will use that money to control the media, the news organizations, the voting procedures and the propaganda. In America the people have the power, and what the majority of the people wish must become law. It may take time, but the people will prevail. Conservatism and Right Wing ideology is now the minority in the US and as of now more minorities are being born than whites. This trend will continue and over time their voices will be heard over the objections of the dinosaurs that currently roam the plains.

Libertarians, no, not the Rand Paul style of fake libertarianism which has become popular within the GOP lately, but the collection of people who are not tied to one political party or another. These are voters who reject the concepts of endless war and warrant less surveillance signed off on by the majority of Republicans as well as many Democrats. They may not be libertarians in the most ideologically pure manner, but there are some voters who believe both in affordable or even free healthcare for all and the right for law-abiding citizens to keep and bear arms, within reason.

The Tea Party. When you allow extremist factions greater power in order to keep votes and donations coming in, eventually something goes wrong. Remember, these aren't people who can be reasoned or bargained with. They view the federal government, our national credit rating, and the world's economy as hostages to be taken and used as negotiating tools in exchange for pushing their agenda, which even includes disenfranchising female voters.

Greed. Sheer, unadulterated greed. For years we've been told that with more corporate profit's, the wealth would eventually "trickle down." Yet with the current economic status of the middle class and record corporate earnings, we can finally dismiss trickle down economics as being the load of bull crap that it really is. Supply side economics is not sustainable. Eventually you run out of natural resources. When people are in dire strait's they just will not buy the disposable garbage that manufacturers make and market.

Lack of Progress. Despite everything the GOP has done to try to stifle the growth of third parties and keep minorities from voting, it's not like Hans Brinker sticking his finger in that Dutch dike to keep the sea from swallowing everything. Eventually, they will lose. Old ideas fall by the wayside. Old prejudices die out with the people who hold them. Putting superstition above science has not worked. Denying Climate Change as a hoax has not played well with anyone with a brain. The younger generations have a trust of science and mathematics that the older generations may not have had. Large majorities know that pollution is bad, no matter how much lipstick you try and put on it. Now that extremists are pushing an agenda of Religion and Creationism should be taught in school instead of Science. The end is surely neigh.

Demographics! Demographics! Demographics! Women are now the largest single voting group in America. They make up over 66% of all voters. With all of the anti abortion over reach going on in the House and in Red States across the US, The Republicans have "Awakened a sleeping giant". Most woman are pro choice and pro contraception. It's estimated that up to 98% of all Catholic Women have used contraception at least once in their lifetime. This is the one demographic where Republicans will lose even with the older generations as they remember quite well their Mothers and Grandmothers fighting for abortion rights back in the 1960s, along with access to contraceptives like the pill. Seriously, does anyone think that "Forced Ultrasounds", denying access to contraceptives, redefining "Rape", defunding Planned Parenthood, closing abortion clinics, and changing the laws that allow Women to make decisions about their own bodies is going to win over women's hearts and minds. I don't think so, in fact, The Republicans should expect the exact opposite effect. Women are pissed off, and very much so in the Red States where bills were put forth and laws changed. Women have an incredibly powerful word of mouth communications network that can overcome anything. Just think about the Texting, Tweeting, and Face Booking going on right now. "Hell hath no Fury"...

Young people and voters under 30 are another large growing electoral group, they are overwhelmingly Liberal, maybe up to 75% or more. Every year, new voters join the rolls and every year, older voters leave the rolls due to the eventual march of time and mortality. Younger voters don't remember the days before desegregation, and they're not as likely to respond positively to the racial, homophobic or xenophobic "dog whistles" used by candidates or media pundit's. They are active in their communities, and they are tech savvy. Their communications skills are unrivaled in human history. They are becoming politically aware at younger and younger ages. They have no jobs, are being forced to work as inters for free, have seen their college tuition costs rise again and again, their student loans become more expensive, and their job prospects after graduation disappear. This group is the least prejudiced among all the groups. To them it doesn't matter what color you are, your religion, or lack thereof, or what your sexual orientation is. They have seen wave after wave of Republican lawmakers try and keep them from voting, Voter ID Laws that do not include School IDs or Military IDs, bills to remove polling from their colleges. Laws to limit their voter registration drives. This is their brave new world, where limitations are accepted challenges to overcome.

A line from an old David Bowie song comes to mind;
"And these children that you spit on
As they try to change their worlds
Are immune to your consultations
They're quite aware of what they're going through".

The LGBT community is a constant in the modern universe. This is their decade, they are a fine tuned Political machine, well oiled, and well funded. Recently a wave of political wins have been fought tooth and nail by Conservatives and Republicans alike. Issues like "Don't ask, don't tell", Marriage equality, equal rights under the law, Anti-Hate laws, and Partner benefit's. The SCOTUS rulings on Prop 8 and DOMA have them energized Nationwide like never before. Polling has showed an ever evolving support for them in the US, where a decade or so ago only 32% of Americans were pro Marriage equality, and Today that number is closer to 60% and gaining more and more every day. Statistically science tells us that 11% of any population is Bi-sexual or Homosexual, however many are still closeted, so the debatable number is lower, maybe 7% or 8%, but one never knows how someone actually votes behind the curtain.

Blacks, or African Americans have been politically energized by a different catalyst. They have now seen a Black President elected with their own eyes. A paradigm that now says to them "Your vote actually does count". Disenfranchised black voters have come out to vote in ever larger numbers and they are most certainly Liberal. In the last election well over 90% voted Democrat. They have taken advantage of early voting and organizing field trips through their churches and civil groups to make sure that anyone in their community that wants to vote can. Transportation is arranged, and they are pre-determined to endure whatever political slowdown or hurdle is put in their way. Surely there have been plenty, Gerrymandered districts, reductions in early voting, Voter ID laws, shenanigans with voting machine access in their districts, billboards warning them of possible criminal activity on their part in the process. There is no doubt in anyone's mind that the Republican Party is Racist, and will continue to be racist. With the SCOTUS ruling gutting the

1964 Voting Act Southern Red States have immediately pushed forth an aggressive agenda of Jim Crow laws designed specifically to limit Black and minority voters. This is an old political fight about to be revisited with modern weapons. Do not underestimate the Cell Phone, Twitter, and Face Book as political weapons of mass media. There is much, much better organization now, groups like the NAACP will lay out the legal arguments and fund the campaigns. The local civic groups and the churches will call the charge.

Latino's are the fastest growing demographic in the Country. Their sheer numbers alone can change the landscape. 72% voted Democrat in the last election. Nearly all are Christian and believe in large families, however they understand perfectly well that Republicans do not aspire to Christian ideals. Families are divided by current Conservative policies, something which they cannot abide. They may be Christian, but like choice and contraception. Latinos have been profiled, discriminated against, scapegoated, mistreated, and in general taken advantage of. Most are very proud of their heritage, and see anti-immigration as an affront to them all. They too have seen a political awakening as many Latino candidates have won Congressional seats and local elections, and Governorships. Sheriff Joe Arpaio has no doubt brought more Latino voters to the polls than any other issue.

Asians are another very rapidly growing group that has seen it's share of disillusion in their community. You should not think of Asians as just another minority, like their Latino brethren, Asians are more communitarian and voted 73% Democrat, in even higher numbers than Latino's. They too, are concerned with immigration reform. Asians account for only three percent of the total vote, they have consistency added well over a half million new voters per cycle. That works out to be close to one half percent gain each time. When you consider that many elections are won or lost on much smaller than three percent, Asians may in time be the deciding factor. One last thing about the Asian demographic is that once they vote they continue to vote with very high participation rates.

Atheists are another incredibly fast growing demographic, where as up until just a few years ago less than 9% of Americans identified as Atheist, Agnostic, or Non Religious. This has changed, and changed dramatically. Recent polling has shown that a minimum of 15% now fall into this group, while some organizations claim that the actual numbers could be as high as 20% to 22%. Many States have much larger percentages than the norm with Vermont, New Hampshire, Wyoming, Alaska, Maine,

Washington, Nevada, Oregon, Delaware, Idaho, and Massachusetts well above the national average. In Vermont for instance 34% of Voters identify as non-religious. Non believers look for substance and scientific fact rather than beliefs or ideology for their opinions. They tend to be for human rights and flat out reject anything non fact or logic based. While on the other side of the coin, people that identify as religious and or Christian, has dropped, also by large numbers from over 90% to approximately 73%. Less and less of us go to Church or other religious meetings each year. It is fairly obvious why this demographic would vote overwhelmingly Liberal. Republicans have entrenched themselves with the Religious Right and Christian law ideology.

Jews know persecution by the Christians and they do not agree with Christian Right ideology. They are overwhelmingly urban and live in large cities, cities that are generally very much Liberal. Why would they vote for a party that is extremely pro Christian, pro gun, anti abortion, and that largely represent rural Evangelicals? The Jewish community is very close and very well organized. They tend to be less split come election day, rather voting more in unison for what best benefit's their community. They voted seventy percent for President Obama, and in higher numbers for Democrats overall. Jews are less than two percent of the overall population, but that is well within the deciding margin of most elections.

Muslims vote overwhelmingly against Republicans, I describe it this way because theoretically they are similar. Both Republicans and Muslims are Conservative. Christian Law and Sharia Law are almost Identical, both religions are against adultery, abortion, pornography, homosexuality, contraception, gambling, consuming alcohol. Both Religions are pro prayer, pro tithing, pro pilgrimage, for God or Allah's law and use water for purification. if you go by the Old Testament penalties, they are identical. Death in all instances of infraction. In another universe they would be a complimentary voting group. Now consider the constant attacks of Islam by the Republicans, discrimination, and Islamophobia, base hatred that Conservatives have shown again, and again. Hundreds of anti Sharia laws and anti Islamic legislation, as well as public disdain of Islam as a secondary, lesser, or primitive religion. Factor in also the Neoconservative initiatives in the middle east against Muslims, like the Drone program, and occupations and/or bases in Saudi Arabia, Iraq, Afghanistan, two basiclly anti Islamic wars, and the Right Wing super pro Israel rhetoric, and there you have it. The results are clear, In 2000 over 70% of Muslims voted for GW Bush, in the last election 85% voted for President Obama.

Non Christians other than the Jews and Muslims like Buddhist's, Hindu's, Wiccan's, etc. also have a disdain for Republicans. Many feel that Republican rhetoric is not inclusive to them, mostly that is true. Everyday Republicans spout more and more Right Wing Evangelical Christian ideology, as well as push Christian law legislation. So anyone who is not of the Christian religion has to feel excluded. Many in this group are also concerned about immigration issues. Minority religions vote a majority for Liberals.

Middle Class Workers and Union members have been alienated at every turn. Overwhelming legislation to pare back Unions, Collective Bargaining, Pension Benefit's, or outright Union Busting have contributed. Right to Work Legislation has been championed or passed in many Republican controlled States. Austerity measures have caused massive layoffs and pain for this demographic. The rhetoric suggests that union members like Police, Firemen, Nurses, Teachers, etc... Are the problem. Public sector unions have borne the brunt of a Conservative push out both in words and deeds. What the GOP doesn't seem to understand is that this is the majority of America. Every family in the last two generations has had a member who has gained from a Union job, or Union benefit's. Wages are stagnant under Republican policies. Wages have gone down quite a bit in "Right to

Work" States. At the same time the wealthy and Corporations have gotten all the breaks, benefit's and money. Continuous efforts of the GOP for upper crust tax breaks, corporate loopholes, and off shoring jobs to increase profit's have taken a huge toll. People are just so done with these policies which have been proven bogus time and time again. Trickle down economics is now recognized as a scam against the average worker for the benefit of the rich. Republicans have done absolutely zero to help the American worker. Not a single jobs bill has been put forth by the GOP controlled house. No raise in the minimum wage. No insentivization of companies to hire. Rather the feeling on the street is that their policies have been designed to work against the common man to benefit the wealthy. A direct result of this disenfranchisement has been a steady drop in the rolls of voters identifying themselves as Republicans. The number of defections have been a very steady 3% per election cycle. Make no mistake, the Republican base is declining at an alarming rate. Another factor contributing to this effect is that older, more Conservative Americans are increasingly older, infirm, and can no longer participate. Or are simply dying off over time.

The Poor, the Elderly, and the Disabled, have come under constant attack through Right wing legislation to pare back any and all social support they have left. We have seen bills proposed to cut Government spending on Social Security, Medicare, Medicaid, Woman's Health, Welfare, Food Stamps, WIC, Education, Public Housing, The GI Bill, Veterans Benefit's, Unemployment, Child Care, Pell Grants, and Student Loans. I am sure there are many others I have not listed. This demographic has clearly been in the cross hairs of the Republicans in thought word, and deed. Their rhetoric has demonized them, calling them Welfare Queens, Moochers, Takers, Leaches, and every other colloquialism you can think of. Don't think that the hypocrisy falls short here. By ostracizing this group the Republicans have surely proven that they are in fact not Christian after all, rather a politicized bastardization in name only.

Ted Cruz, Yes, Ted Cruz. Sure there are other nut jobs that have driven the GOP close to going over the ideological cliff, but Ted Cruz reminds me of Major Kong riding a falling hydrogen bomb in the famous movie "Dr. Strangelove." No single politician wanted it as badly and did more to ensure the government's shutdown than Ted Cruz. Just like Major Kong, he's whooping and hollering all the way to oblivion, to the end of the Republican Party and there's nothing they can do about it. Republicans have truly let the patients take over the asylum. Cruz is not the only wing ding in the party. They have trotted out so many

Wackadoo's lately that the list seems more like a "Who's Who" of Bigotry, Racism, Misogyny, Ignorance, and just plain old stupidity. The likes of Sarah Palin, Michelle Bachman, Joe Walsh, Eric Cantor, Allen West, Louis Gohmert, Mike Lee, Ted Yoho, Steve King, Pete Hoekstra, Susan Angle, Christine O'Donnell, Connie Mack, Paul Brown, Virginia Foxx, Pat Toomey, Joe Wilson... And the list goes on and on... You get the picture.

In conclusion, the evidence is most profound in the Great State of Texas where the minority population is increasing faster than just about anywhere else. The trend in Texas is that the Republicans are losing ground steadily election cycle after election cycle. Within the next three cycles Texas will go from Red to Purple to Blue. Once that happens, No Republican will ever again be President of the United States. The combination of New York, California, and Texas will cause a Democratic electoral majority. Or at least no Republican who promotes the current platform.

Republicans are Fascists

The 14 Characteristics of Fascism as related to the Conservative Movement and the Republican Party in the United States.

I used a modified version of;
"The 14 Characteristics of Fascism" by Political scientist Dr. Lawrence Britt for this article.
Originally published in Free Inquiry Magazine in 2003

1. Powerful and Continuing Nationalism Fascist regimes tend to make constant use of patriotic motto's, slogans, symbols, songs, and other paraphernalia. Flags are seen everywhere, as are flag symbols on clothing and in public displays.
Republicans point out every and any actual and or perceived disrespect to our flag.
Republicans always wear flag pins, and try to discredit those that don't.
Disrespect for anyone not acting as patriotic as they are, even if they are within their rights.
Condescending to any contradiction or critique of their patriotism.
Zero tolerance of any dissenting opinion.
Voting again and again on our motto of "In God we Trust", for repeal of the American Health Act, or for increased anti abortion bill, person hood, district Gerrymandering, voter ID laws, etc... Even if they have zero chance of passing. Saying

over and over that the voters are confused and don't really understand the issue, inferring that anyone not voting for these issues is somehow Un-American, Un-Patriotic, Socialist, Communist, or Treasonous.

Case in point was when Rick Perry accused Ben Bernanke of Treason if he allowed more quantitative easing.

2. Disdain for the Recognition of Human Rights Because of fear of enemies and the need for security, the people in fascist regimes are persuaded that human rights can be ignored in certain cases because of "need". The people tend to look the other way or even approve of torture, summary executions, assassinations, long incarcerations of prisoners, etc.

Republicans demonize the poor, the sick, women, and anyone who receives any monetary help from the government.

Republicans have demonstrated that they are willing to torture to protect the US.

Republicans Initiated and still fight continuously for the continual detention of prisoners in Guantanamo Bay Cuba.

Extreme Rendition.

The Patriot Act.

The Bush Doctrine.

Continual votes on repeal of the American Health Act, and against any bill that may even slightly infringe on Corporate profit's in the private sector.

3. Identification of Enemies/Scapegoats as a Unifying Cause The people are rallied into a unifying patriotic frenzy over the need to eliminate a perceived common threat or foe: racial , ethnic or religious minorities; liberals; communists; socialists, terrorists, etc.

Republicans blame everyone for the ills of the country except themselves.

Socialists

Communists

Marxists

Welfare recipients

Women

Children

Druggies

Moochers

Takers

Minorities

Immigrants

Liberals

Democrats

Unions

Terrorists

Muslims

Foreigners

They use code words and phrases that are racist and misogynist in their rhetoric and propaganda

Let's be honest here, who don't they blame?

4. Supremacy of the Military even when there are widespread domestic problems, the military is

given a disproportionate amount of government funding, and the domestic agenda is neglected. Soldiers and military service are glamorized.

Increased Military budget every year since 1980 Republican overspending on Military projects.

Republican professed love for the troops and National Defense

Republicans Promotion of War and military action to the detriment of the US Economy.

Wars in Afghanistan and Iraq.

Republican agenda to eliminate all other Government agencies other than Military or Military support roles. Example, the creation of the Department of Homeland Defense and wanting to eliminate the EPA, Dept of Education, Dept of Energy, etc...

Republicans work tirelessly to eliminate Welfare, Food Stamps, Unemployment, Planned Parenthood, etc...

voting to fund double and triple redundant Military suppliers

promoting ludicrous Military programs even when completely unnecessary

Promoting limited or no oversight of military spending because of national security. They truly believe that the individual citizens should not know how much is being spent because of super secret military programs that will keep us safe somehow, even if we don't know what they are. They will even go so far as to say that those $4000 "Toilets" or $1000 "Hammers" are the only way to fund those super secret programs that they can't tell us about.

5. Rampant Sexism the governments of fascist nations tend to be almost exclusively male-dominated. Under fascist regimes, traditional gender roles are made more rigid. Divorce, abortion and homosexuality are suppressed and the state is represented as the ultimate guardian of the family institution.
Republicans have pushed over 300 bills dedicated to the elimination of Abortion
Republicans have been pushing Family Values in Government for years. Anti Divorce, Anti Abortion, Anti Gay.
Constant promotion of traditional "Family Values"
Support of the Religious Right in all matters.
Pushing for Constitutional Amendments to implement Extremist Christian values on abortion, contraception, person hood, anti gay rights, anti woman rights.
Republicans are against Gay rights and Gay marriage in every instance
against the repeal of Don't ask, don't tell in the Military.
Anti contraceptive
anti women rights
voting against pre-K funding
voting against contraceptive funding
voting against abortion in all instances
voting against federal money for any women's

health issues
voting against violence against woman act
voting against equal pay for equal work legislation
continual support of DOMA

6. Controlled Mass Media Sometimes to media is directly controlled by the government, but in other cases, the media is indirectly controlled by government regulation, or sympathetic media spokespeople and executives. Censorship, especially in war time, is very common.
Conservative Media Organizations: Certain conservative media outlets such as NewsMax, WorldNetDaily, and Fox News describe themselves as news organizations, but are generally seen as promoting a conservative agenda. News Corp's Corporate ownership of media and news organizations have been politicized, Fox news is now a direct propaganda arm of the Republican party.
News Corp bought the Wall Street Journal
Forbes is pro Republican.
Multiple other fake news outlets and blogs like Breitbart, Drudge, Rush Limbaugh, Glen Beck, etc... actively push the Rights agenda through lies and manipulation.
PAC and SuperPAC money being raised to play Republican propaganda and lies on all major networks and cable.
Media Concentration: A handful of corporate

conglomerates (example, (Disney, CBS Corporation, News Corporation, TimeWarner, and General Electric) own the majority of mass media outlets in the United States. Such a uniformity of ownership means that stories which are critical of these corporations may often be underplayed in the media.

Capitalist Model: In the United States the media are operated for profit, and are usually funded by advertising. Stories critical of advertisers or their interests may in some cases be underplayed, while stories favorable to advertisers may be given more coverage.

7. Obsession with National Security Fear is used as a motivational tool by the government over the masses.

Republicans are true fear mongers;

Drugs

Immigrants

Minorities

Terrorists

Liberals

Socialists

Communists

Marxists

Unions

Muslims

Conspiracy theory's abound on everything

Gay rights: "gays will harm your children," and "gays who raise children are more likely to raise gays, and this is clearly bad for children." The very loaded term "defense" of marriage is at the core of the politics of fear. You need only defend against that which attacks you. "Gays who are allowed to marry will destroy the value of your marriage: Defend Marriage!"

Less powerful, but tried never the less, is the use of the term "Nazi" to instill fear of feminists. Empowered women will take away your jobs even though they are unqualified because of some silly "equality in hiring" laws.

Mexicans, or "illegals," are out to "take your jobs," and "destroy all you know of your land," and "Force you to speak Spanish." These examples, while not as powerful a fear tactic, still rely on loaded language to associate fearful things with whatever the target is. Similarly, African Americans use affirmative action to take your jobs – and even get their ideas into politics.

8. Religion and Government are Intertwined
Governments in fascist nations tend to use the most common religion in the nation as a tool to manipulate public opinion. Religious rhetoric and terminology is common from government leaders, even when the major tenets of the religion are diametrically opposed to the government's policies or actions.
Republicans are in bed with the Catholics, the Evangelicals, and the Baptists

Use every Biblical reference they can find to support their versions of events and issues.

They point to the Bible as the rule and guide to support that they have God on their side even if the Bible says nothing about the issue.

Have been pushing a rigid religious right agenda, more and more politicalization of churches and religious groups, christian media like The 700 Club, Christian Broadcasting Network continual support of Republicans

Claims of secularism or Separation of Church and State are attacks against Freedom of Religion, and/or Christians.

Constant push of Religious values as overwhelmingly the majority opinion, or that Christian law is somehow higher than civilian or federal law.

9. Corporate Power is Protected The industrial and business aristocracy of a fascist nation often are the ones who put the government leaders into power, creating a mutually beneficial business/government relationship and power elite.

Protect the "Job Creators" at all costs, and every instance

constant reduction of taxes for corporations

loopholes for corporations, not just direct subsidies for big oil, farms, agriculture, health insurers, or private jets. But the formation of Real Estate Investment Trusts, Master Limited

Partnerships, Limited Partnerships and Hybrids that pay zero federal taxes. Subsidies for corporations and the wealthy, Ethanol and Farm subsidies, Oil & Gas Subsidies, Banking and Insurance Subsidies. These Corporations make Billions in profit's and corporate profit's have increased exponentially as of late and are now the highest in our history.

non prosecution of corporations and the wealthy, No banks, bankers, Insurance companies, their employees, credit rating agencies or their employees, etc... Have been prosecuted or jailed as a result of the recession.

bailouts for corporations and the wealthy, TARP, TALF, etc... Reducing the Fed discount rate to zero allowing banks to borrow at taxpayer expense at zero to 0.25 basis points for years. When was the last time you were able to get an indefinite loan at lets say 0.12% ?

10. Labor Power is Suppressed Because the organizing power of labor is the only real threat to a fascist government, labor unions are either eliminated entirely, or are severely suppressed.
Have actively demonized public and private unions
pushed "Right to Work" agenda nationwide
opposed laws to make unionization easier
trying to destroy the US Post Office Union
Union busting at the state level, remember Ohio SB5?

148

Corporations spend Billions annually to help Republicans suppress unions, people like the Koch Brothers give quite generously with this specific request.

11. Disdain for Intellectuals and the Arts Fascist nations tend to promote and tolerate open hostility to higher education, and academia. It is not uncommon for professors and other academics to be censored or even arrested. Free expression in the arts and letters is openly attacked.

Attacking Democrats, celebrities, and Liberals as "Elitists"

attacking academics and professors as Elitists and Socialists

attacking economists directly, providing alternate theories of economics

suppression of NASA Scientists writings and publishing

Climate change is a hoax

hydraulic fracturing or fracking dangers as a hoax

legislating for more drilling on public lands and parks

legislating cuts to PBS, and the arts nationwide as wasteful spending under the guise of fiscal responsibility

12. Obsession with Crime and Punishment Under fascist regimes, the police are given

almost limitless power to enforce laws. The people are often willing to overlook police abuses and even forgo civil liberties in the name of patriotism. There is often a national police force with virtually unlimited power in fascist nations. Constant profession of law and order in society, blame of criminals and massive incarceration rates, incarceration as voter suppression of minorities, incarceration as suppression of opposing ideas, increased suppression of constitutional rights under the guise of terrorism, wireless wiretaps, rendition, stop loss, suspension of due process and habeas corpus under the patriot act, hell, the whole Patriot Act, police brutality and beating of journalists and protesters, unlawful arrest of journalists and protesters, unlawful prosecution of journalists and protesters.

The US is the largest per capita imprisoned group in the world, more of our citizens are incarcerated, and stripped of their voting rights that anywhere else on earth, while at the same time we profess others improve their human rights records. We scream about prison camps in North Korea, China, Russia, etc... All the while we have privatized our prisons and made them for profit with taxpayer dollars. In-proportionately large numbers of minorities, blacks and Latinos especially are incarcerated under this system. Stop and frisk policies of minorities

Active Racial profiling

Arrest, suppression, and physical abuse of Journalists and student activists.

Not to mention how the police actively beat and pepper spray passive protests at schools and at Occupy protests. This is just as wrong as what happened in Selma Alabama in 1965, only now the aggressors are attacking anyone who disagrees with their ideas and policies.

Militarization of police forces around the country, exponential use of SWAT teams.

13. Rampant Cronyism and Corruption Fascist regimes almost always are governed by groups of friends and associates who appoint each other to government positions and use governmental power and authority to protect their friends from accountability. It is not uncommon in fascist regimes for national resources and even treasures to be appropriated or even outright stolen by government leaders.

Lobbying of congress by the banking, oil, coal, gas, pharmaceutical, gun, insurance, prison, auto, steel, restaurant, and every other damn industry

PACs, Super PACs, and direct donations in excess by corporations and others

Citizens United ruling allowing excessive money into the political process

Appointing hacks, fake experts, lobbyists, family, friends, donors, etc... after winning an election.

No bid contracts, some ridiculous percentage like 60% of all Military contracts are just given out with no bidding process.

Privatization is the largest group in terms of corruption, what the government did previously for $1 privatization now cost the taxpayer tenfold. Privatization of many Military functions is now commonplace, we used to have enlisted soldiers cook meals, now they are catered. The army core of engineers and the Sea Bees used to build roads, bridges, tunnels, structures, etc... Now all private. All at far greater cost than before. Prisons, waste removal, paperwork, latrines, airstrips, maintenance duties, and so much more. Private security companies abound, think "Blackwater" who do as they want, charge what they want, lobby as they wish, and bill the taxpayer Billions...

14. Fraudulent Elections Sometimes elections in fascist nations are a complete sham. Other times elections are manipulated each and every time by the use of smear tactics, campaigns against or even assassination of character of opposition candidates. They use legislation to control voting numbers or political district boundaries, and manipulation of the media. Fascist nations also typically use their judiciaries to manipulate or control elections.

Voter suppression thru unconstitutional voter id legislation

Voter suppression by means of restricting early voting and absentee voting

Voter suppression thru intimidation

Voter suppression thru Gerrymandering

Voter suppression thru redefining and/or changing electoral district laws

Voter suppression thru changes to registration rules

Voter suppression thru registration omission or fraud

Constant proposals for end runs around Jim Crow laws

Voter suppression thru manipulating electronic votes

thru allocation of state voting machines to preferred districts
Thru manipulation and creating extremely long wait's in non preferred districts

Defunding of Public Education

School Vouchers, another really bad Republican Idea

Republicans are always going on about school vouchers for private schools. It is absolutely part of their platform and talking points to privatize education. Their view is that the vouchers would be used to send kids to Catholic School or some other Christian school. They believe it furthers their "Religious Right" agenda. It funnels public money to Christian churches and schools.

I have to now poke some pretty big holes in their plan. In order for School vouchers to be constitutional vouchers would need to be available to all private schools. So they could be used for an Islamic Fundamental school, or a Pagan School. Certainly for Jewish schools. If School Vouchers becomes the law of the land theoretically foreign money could come to the US to open all kinds of alternate private schools and would then be funded by public money. Seriously Do you want your tax money funding a thousand Muslim Medrassas? I didn't think so.

Unconstitutional, Since most of the schools in the program are religious, government funding violates the First Amendment and the concept of Separation of Church and State. About 85 percent of private schools are religious. Vouchers tend to be a means of circumventing the Constitutional prohibitions against subsidizing religious practice and instruction. The vast majority of private schools are run by religious groups. According to the U.S. Department of Education, 76 percent of private schools have a religious affiliation. Over 80 percent of students attending private schools are enrolled in religious institutions. Most of these religious schools seek to indoctrinate as well as educate. They integrate religion throughout their curriculum and often require all students to receive religious instruction and attend religious services. Thus, there is no way to prevent publicly funded vouchers from paying for these institutions' religious activities and education.

In other words, vouchers force Americans to pay taxes to support religion. This runs counter to the First Amendment's guarantee of religious liberty. In America, all religious activities should be supported with voluntary contributions. James Madison, Thomas Jefferson and other Founders strongly supported the separation of church and state and opposed taxation to support religion. As Ben Franklin succinctly put it: "When a religion is good, I conceive it will support itself; and when it does not support itself, and God does not care to support it, so that it's professors are obliged to call for the help of the civil power, 'tis a sign, I apprehend, of it's being a bad one." School vouchers are little more than a backdoor way for the government to subsidize religious and other private schools. With most voucher bills, private schools can accept tax money and still deny admission to any student they decide. Unlike public schools, private schools can and do discriminate against students based on various criteria, including religion, disability, economic background, academic record, English language ability or disciplinary history. Public funds should pay only for public schools that are open to all children and accountable to the people. Private schools are also free to impose religious criteria on teachers and staff. Teachers at religious schools have been fired for having the "wrong" views about religion, for marrying someone of another faith, for getting divorced, for being gay and even for taking public stands that conflict with the church's view. This may be legal, but it shouldn't be subsidized by taxpayers.

Voucher advocates say that the Supreme Court ruled in Zelman v. Simmons-Harris, 2002 that Cleveland's voucher program did not violate the church state provisions of the Constitution. This is true, but the advocates overlook an important fact, the Zelman case did not address state constitutional issues. Some three dozen states have church state provisions in their constitutions that are even stronger than the US Constitution.

These provisions often more explicitly bar taxpayer money from being used to fund religious schools and education. Private school vouchers would likely be unconstitutional in most states, and some state courts have already ruled that they are unconstitutional.

Vouchers take money away from Public Schools that are already way under funded.

Public schools must accept everyone regardless of disabilities, test scores, religion, or other characteristics; private schools can show favoritism or discrimination in selecting students. Many studies, like those administered by the National Assessment of Educational Progress, indicate that public schools are generally on equal footing with private schools. Students doing the same coursework perform about equally in both institutions. Studies which show different tend to omit factors like income level, education level of parents, learning disabilities, etc... When these things are taken into account, we get a different picture and this shows that private schools aren't really any better than public schools. Studies also show that the students who do best are those whose parents are the most actively involved in their children's education, something vouchers won't change. The idea that public schools are failing is a myth, but not supported by facts. If we look at long term trends reported by the National Assessment of Educational Progress, commonly referred to as "The Nation's Report Card", we find that reading scores for 17 year old's were the same in 1999 as in 1973. That's pretty impressive in a culture turning increasingly towards visual entertainment. Math scores have actually improved over those than in the early 1970s and science scores, which dropped from 1969-82, are getting strong again.

Vouchers do not decrease education costs. Instead, tax money that would ordinarily go to public schools now pays for vouchers, thus harming public schools. A 1999 study of Cleveland's program showed that the public schools from which students left for private voucher schools were spread throughout the district. The loss of a few students at a school does not reduce fixed costs such as teacher salaries, textbooks and supplies and utilities and maintenance costs. Public schools run the risk of losing state funding to pay for vouchers without being able to cut their overall operating costs. In addition, voucher programs cost the state money to administer. In Milwaukee, which has been disproportionately burdened in a statewide voucher funding scheme, the city has had to raise property taxes several times since the voucher program began in order to ensure adequate funding for the city's schools.

The quality of education at the private schools may be brought down by new students that aren't as gifted.

Where vouchers are in place such as Milwaukee, Cleveland, and Florida, a two-tiered system has been set up that holds students in public and private schools to different standards.

Vouchers were not designed to help low income children. Milton Friedman, the "grandfather" of vouchers, dismissed the notion that vouchers could help low income families, saying "it is essential that no conditions be attached to the acceptance of vouchers that interfere with the freedom of private enterprises to experiment."

A pure voucher system would only encourage economic, racial, ethnic, and religious stratification in our society. America's success has been built on our ability to unify our diverse populations.

Most Americans are against Vouchers and have said so in the polls. When people are asked to vote directly on vouchers at actual elections, they always reject them by wide margins. Since 1967, voters in twenty three states have said "NO" to vouchers, public money, and tax aid to religious and private schools at the voting booth.
According to multiple studies of the District of

Columbia, Milwaukee and Cleveland school voucher programs, the targeted population does not perform better in reading and math than students in public schools. The U.S. Department of Education studies of the D.C. program show that the students using vouchers to attend private schools do not believe that their voucher school is better or safer than the public school they left.

The study also showed that over a period of four years, there was no statistically significant difference between students who were offered a voucher and those who were not in their aspirations for future schooling, engagement in extracurricular activities, frequency of doing homework, attendance at school, reading for enjoyment or tardiness rates. In fact, students who participated in the program may actually have been more likely to be absent from school. Likewise, there was no significant difference in the student-teacher ratios in their classrooms or the availability of before and after school programs in their schools.

Vouchers don't help the poor because they generally do not cover the whole tuition cost, or the school fees. Only families with the means to pay the difference of the rest of the tuition, uniforms, transportation, books and supplies benefit from them. In Cleveland, the majority of families who were given a voucher but did not use it said the additional costs were the reason they could not use them. Vouchers actually hurt low income families by undermining the public schools they rely on.

Private schools aren't subject to as rigorous of oversight, other than from the market for schools and they may not act responsibly.

Private schools are free to pick and choose whomever they wish as students, freely discriminating for reasons of race, religion, disability, cost to educate, whatever, they can refuse admission or expel students for any reason whatsoever. Public schools must, except in extreme cases, accept whomever wishes to apply, including those with expensive physical or learning disabilities, behavioral disorders, contagious diseases, or language deficiencies. Most private schools can avoid the costs and problems of educating unusual and special needs students. This is one way that voucher advocates can claim that the per capita education costs are lower at private schools than at public schools. Voucher programs do not increase "choice" for parents because it's the private schools that will ultimately decide whether to admit a student. These institutions are not required to give parents the information necessary to determine whether the school is meeting their children's needs. Under voucher programs, private schools are sometimes not required to test students, publish curriculum or meet many other standards. Even when legislatures have attempted to mandate accountability standards in voucher programs, private schools have ignored their responsibilities.

Scams abound in Milwaukee and Cleveland, the availability of vouchers led con artists to create fly by night schools in order to bilk the public purse. One Milwaukee school was run by a known criminal. In Cleveland, a school operated out of a sub par building with lousy heat and no fire alarms. Another school "educated" children by having them watch videos all day.

Fundamentalist Christian schools have been growing rapidly in number. Many of these schools offer education way outside the mainstream. They teach creationism instead of evolution, or science. They teach bogus "Christian Nation" history instead of American history and put out wacky ideas about other religions, the role of women, gay rights and other issues. These schools may legally teach this way, but taxpayers should not pay for it. Fundamentalist Islamic Schools certainly could be a tax payer funded reality.

Extremist or strange religious or political, cults,

and even hucksters may be allowed to operate schools and receive public money for doing so. Immune from government oversight, they would be free to pursue whatever goals they may have, even including child abuse. The only way to avoid this is to subject schools which receive vouchers to very strict regulations. That, however, would force the government to become more deeply involved with religion than is constitutional, the more regulations and restrictions which are imposed on private schools, the less different they will be from public schools, this undermines some of the reasons for vouchers in the first place.

Voucher plans usually allow a small percentage of children to leave public schools for enrollment in private schools. This does nothing for the large percentage of youngsters left behind. Most public schools do a very good job; those that don't should be fixed, not abandoned. Vouchers become an excuse for politicians to dodge issues like adequate funding, class size, teacher training and curriculum reform.

Although it would be nice for poor children to attend good private schools if the parents wish, that doesn't mean that it is the government's responsibility to fund it. Insofar as the government has an obligation to see that everyone gets a basic education, that is fulfilled by the public schools. If private schools want to have those children, they can offer scholarships, as many already do.

If you want private schools to survive, then donate money to them, at no point is it necessary for the government to subsidize the education of specific students there. People who really do value the free market will recognize that the survival of such schools are not automatically the responsibility of the government.

Voucher schemes will force the government to subsidize the cost of education for students already attending private schools. That would cost the taxpayers billions of extra dollars. Why should we as taxpayers pay for someone else's private school education?

Free market competition makes non competitive industries improve or die, but the idea of the free market improving an industry depends on their being real competition, but there is no real competition between public and private schools. Public schools must fund the transportation of students, whereas private schools don't have to. Public schools must follow government regulations on how to treat children, how to maintain buildings, treat race, religion, disabilities, etc... Private schools have few restrictions to follow, especially religious schools.

Voucher funding is done by taking money out of public education budgets, these budgets are usually sadly underfunded to begin with. This Causes cuts to transportation, security, improvements, repairs, supplies, and staff. Inner city schools would be hurt the most. There is a great deal of moaning about paying to fund social services which are designed to help the poor. Well off people are always looking for ways to stop contributing to educate poor minorities, part of this creates a permanent minority underclass.

Parents who send their kids to private schools are only taxed once when they pay public school taxes. Private school fees are not a tax, they are a voluntary payment to a private school. Replacing a public service with a private service does not entitle you to a refund. People who hire private security firms do not get money back from the police, people who install private pools do not get refunds for not using public pools, and people who drive cars don't get a dime from public transit. Public services offer benefit's to society as a whole, even those who choose not to use them.

Ninety percent of children in the US attend public schools. We need to focus on fully funding, fixing, and improving this system, not siphoning off money for the privileged class.

Military Spending

Today we hear the word "Socialism" bantered about like it is completely EVIL when in fact, All Democracies, Republics, and Developed Nations are a mix of Capitalism to Communism and Socialism.

I would like to just point out that the US Military is a 100% Socialist organization. 100% Taxpayer Funded Military Socialism includes, but is not limited to;

Free Housing and Free Food, Free Clothes as Uniforms and Boots

Free Healthcare for Life including Vision & Dental because we need healthy warriors

Free Education including College and Graduate school through the Montgomery Act

This is not a Bad thing! It just so confusing when people say Socialism is Bad and yet we must Support the Troops at the same time.

Another thought here on the military budget, most of what used to be considered "Foreign Aid" now falls under the military budget. All of that blather that we constantly hear about sending money to foreign countries is bunk, because if you say a word about cutting the military budget, they will scream "No!, because we must have a strong military to insure peace." Let me lay out the foreign aid in the military budget for you;

China $166 Billion
Russia 91 Billion
Britain $61 Billion
Japan $59 Billion
France $59 Billion
Saudi Arabia $57 Billion
India $46 Billion
Germany $46 Billion
Italy $34 Billion
Brazil $33 Billion
South Korea $32 Billion
Australia $26 Billion
Canada $23 Billion
Turkey $18 Billion
Other Foreign countries not listed $320 Billion
US military $683 Billion

That is a total of approximately $1.75 Trillion dollars. Compare that to the measly $90 Billion for welfare and SNAP combined and basically you are cutting off the parsley to spite the giant steak on the plate.

Note: Numbers rounded to nearest Billion.

Voter ID

Republicans have propagated this idea that voter fraud is rampant and that we must have voter id laws to stop it. That premise is entirely incorrect. The actual number of actual voter fraud cases are statistically near zero. Somewhere between 0.001% and 0.003% is the academic consensus. Yet somehow Conservatives and Republicans have used scare tactics to convince the people of a boogie man that lives at the polls.

The strategic reasoning is simple. Scare the people into voting for something they can use as a tool to win elections. Individual States have carved out nice little niches of law that prevent people from voting, not prevent fraud. It is a pretty sure thing that elections were held for decades and decades since the American revolution. People of yesteryear certainly did not have id, or photo id, and somehow elections were held, people elected and voted out. Life went on.

Today's GOP uses voter ID laws like a surgeons scalpel, carefully crafting out the little groups of the demographic that they know will vote Liberal or Democrat. Students, Women, Minorities, the Elderly Poor, etc... While on the surface voter id seems a reasonable idea, the results are overwhelmingly unfair.

By making College and student Id's ineligible they confuse and eliminate large groups of students. While they will learn the lesson and correct it, one election cycle has gone by without their vote counted. Each cycle will bring another group of new students that will be disenfranchised.

Passing laws that require that the voter registration match exactly the drivers license insures a large percentage of women will be kept out of the voting process. When a woman gets married she usually changes her name taking the last name of her new husband. So if "Mary Ann Jones" married "John Smith", her name might be on her voter registration as "Mary Jones" or "Mary Smith", depending on State law, and, or personal preference her drivers license or state ID may say "Mary Ann Smith", "Mary Jones Smith", "Mary Jones-Smith", etc... The difference of a hyphen or not can be the difference between allowing them to vote or not, even if they fix the discrepancy for the next vote, a new group of newly married women will have to go through it also, and so on.

Back in the 1960s with the advent of the Civil Rights movement the counter movement like the Klu Klux Klan, The Knights of the White Camellia, and just plain racist townsfolk had burned and destroyed black birth records, they burned black hospitals, churches, municipal buildings that may have housed original copies of birth certificates. Then they passed voter id laws that you had to provide your birth certificate in order to vote. Many black people did not have a copy of their birth certificate and could not get a replacement because all of the original were destroyed. In fact many southern blacks today still can not get a certified copy of their birth certificate because of these racist actions half a century ago. This was part of the Jim Crow law strategy. Using legal means to prevent minorities from voting as well as other repressions.

The Voting Rights Act of 1965 had gotten rid of all these racist voter manipulations and the the worst offenders had to get permission form the Federal Department of Justice in order to change their election laws.

Now with SCOTUS striping Article four of the Civil Rights Act most southern states have immediately presented or passed laws similar to those Jim Crow voter laws of the 1960s.

Voter id laws also try to end run around the poll tax ban. Jim Crow laws called for charging a poll tax in order to vote as this discouraged the poor and minorities from voting, other strategies included literacy tests. All of which have since been rendered unconstitutional. Now consider the cause of a 65 year old who has lost or never had their birth certificate. If they can in fact get a certified copy from the municipality where they were born, the town or city will charge a fee, sometimes as high as $25.00 So if you have to pay for something in order to vote, that is a poll tax, and therefore illegal and unconstitutional. Not taking into account how burdensome these requirements are for disabled or elderly people. Texas has so few official voter id locations that even just getting to one is a major hurdle. For a young person without a car, or an elderly person who can no longer drive, this can be quite an event in and of itself

According to studies done by the Brennan center and others roughly 11% of the entire US eligible population could be impacted negatively by these laws. Texas is estimated to have almost 200,000 people without required ID, not counting the whole name has to be exact thing. As of a week before the 2013 elections only about 60 people had actually obtained the new State ID.

The one thing that really sticks in my craw is that while most people without the proper id tend to not vote anyway, they are unknowingly giving up their right to vote. When and if they are motivated to become active at the polls, it wont matter, it will be too late, the damage done. While they will allow you to vote on a provisional ballot in most cases analysis of what happens to those ballots has shown that they are usually just thrown away.

Most State Voter ID laws have been stayed or blocked by Federal judges as unconstitutional. However the perceived public damage has already been done. If people think or believe, even incorrectly, that they can not vote because they don't have the proper ID, they wont go to the polls afraid of prosecution and, or fines. Fear mongering used to maximum advantage. States that have passed some form of Voter ID law after the SCOTUS ruling have found themselves having to defend their law from Federal Department of Justice Law suit's. These lawsuit's will likely win at enormous costs to the individual states. Texas and North Carolina are currently in such predicaments.

Democrats do not like voter ID laws, and fight them at every turn believing that everyone should be allowed to vote and the easier it is to vote the more likely people will participate in the process. Republicans on the other hand are using voter ID to their every advantage at the polls, Red States have been on a virtual mission to pass them. Certainly in close elections they believe voter ID laws will give them an edge.

In conclusion the GOP has created a problem where none existed, fabricated a fake solution to fix the non existent problem, sold a bill of goods to the public and changed the public perception, all for the benefit of their candidates. Seems to me if you can't win an election based on your ideas and the issues your ideas suck. Period.

Gerrymandering

Redistricting is when they move or re-draw the state electoral district borders... This happens right after the new census information comes out. Adjustments of districts should represent the people that live there, especially if there have been big changes in the demographics of the area. This seems basically reasonable and fair, and in fact it should be. Gerrymandering is when a particular political party uses the redistricting process to re-draw the lines so that it give them a political advantage. During the election of 1812 the word "Gerrymander" was used in many Federalist newspapers in New England and nationwide. This pointed to an organized action of the Federalists to beat Governor Elbridge Gerry at that time. Gerrymandering soon began to be used to describe other cases of district manipulation for partisan gain. It is particularly useful in keeping incumbents in office, by locking in their parties demographics solidly in a majority.

Gerrymandering has two basic strategies. One is called "Packing" where you draw the lines so that you put as many friendly voters into a district, and "Cracking" were you spread out unwanted votes thinly among many districts to minimize their actual impact on the elections. Entire districts can be gerrymandered out of existence and making the seat of an actual political rival just go away or disappear. Dennis Kucinich (D-OH) was gerrymandered out of the House of Representatives when his district was re-drawn to have him fight an election against another Democratic candidate where her district was much larger and stronger. Either way the Republicans drew the lines and Ohio lost an entire Democratic district and Congressman. There have been efforts to have districts redrawn by independent non partisan companies or groups, however this concept has not caught on in general. Some states have adopted some parts to be be done independently, they are a definite minority.

With all of this manipulation going on ponders the question why is Gerrymandering still legal? There have been rulings on Gerrymandering and the best information I can glean is that the courts have basically upheld the concept that as long as "the populations must be roughly equal and that that there was not any restriction on the shapes of the districts, so long as they are contiguous".

Of note here is the fact that in the 2012 general elections, Democrats won the popular vote by more than 1.5 million individual votes, and yet the House held on to their Republican majority, solely because of Gerrymandering. The outrageous divergence was more apparent in some Red states and less in others. Hmmm...

Republicans are Terrorists

The Republican De-Evolution from Political Party to Domestic Terrorists 9-22-13 by Allen Clifton

I remember back during the Bush administration, a friend of mine said something along the lines of, "I can't wait till Bush is out of office. Republicans can't get much worse than this." I told him at the time that he shouldn't be so certain of that.

During that time the tea party didn't exist (or at least it had no national popularity) so neither of us had definitive proof that something worse was on the way. However, I've just always lived by the belief that when it comes to politics, it can always get worse.

Being a liberal, it goes without saying that there are very few issues where I find myself agreeing with conservatives. But to look back at their de-evolution from an opposing political party to what now basically amounts to a domestic terrorist organization, is downright shocking.

A few days ago, I wrote an article where I said that Republicans have officially become the "American Taliban." This of course brought out the right-wing trolls who called my claim absurd. Of course, most had no information to support their belief that my claim was false, but that didn't stop them from aggressively bashing the piece.

The stereotype of a terrorist (at least the American stereotype) is some form of Islamic radical who wishes to harm the United States in some way. Most simply equate this to some kind of public explosion or mass killings of Americans.

This, of course, is a completely ignorant, shallow stereotype. There are all forms of terrorism and it doesn't just originate from Islamic radicalism.

So, why can't Republicans be classified as domestic terrorists? Because that sounds too extreme to say? If you believe that I understand, but is it really that extreme of a belief? Is it more extreme than what they've been attempting to do to our nation?

Let's just look at the definition of the word "terrorism."

Terrorism: the use of violence and threats to intimidate or coerce, especially for political purposes, the state of fear and submission produced by terrorism or terrorization, a terroristic method of governing or of resisting a government.

Are Republicans not using threats as a means to coerce government? "Defund Obamacare or else we'll shutdown the government and not raise the debt ceiling!" Both actions would cause massive devastation for millions of Americans and (as it relates to the debt ceiling) quite possibly crash our entire economy.

But that's not a threat? Of course it is. And it's not just a threat, it's a purposeful act which they know will harm millions of Americans. They simply don't care. They have their "demands" they want met, and they don't care who they have to hurt in order to get what they want.

The state of fear and submission? Oh that's easy. Please, outside of straight, white, conservative Christian males, who aren't Republicans afraid of? The Republican party, and the conservative media, constantly perpetuate fear mongering against homosexuals, women, minorities, Muslims, liberals, any media that isn't right-wing approved, Hollywood, science, history, math, education, the poor—hell, they've classified Bill Nye as "liberally biased."

Bill freaking Nye! You really have to be fear mongering to turn a guy mostly known for Saturday morning kids science shows into some kind of political enemy.

Oh, and Obamacare, holy cow. These people are terrified of Obamacare. But can you blame them? Have you seen the kinds of ads right-wing groups are putting out there? Seriously, click that link and go take a look. It's worth your two minutes to see those ridiculous ads funded by the Koch brothers. Nothing quite like a spooky clown-looking version of Uncle Sam appearing between a woman's legs in the middle of an intimate doctor's exam (with creepy music playing in the background) to insinuate that the government is out to inject itself into your privates, uh, I mean private life.

This party thrives on fear. Fear socialism! Fear communism! Fear a dictionary which might inform you of the definitions for both of those economic ideologies! Because most Republicans, as it stands now, sure as heck don't know how to define either.

A terroristic method of governing or of resisting government? Well, let's just go back to their strategy of refusing to do their jobs unless they get their way. Threatening to raise taxes on every American if the top two-percent didn't keep their tax cuts. Threatening to default on our debt in 2011 (and now) by refusing to raise the debt ceiling if they don't get the budget cuts they want. Threatening to shutdown the government (they actually did in the 90's) if the president refuses to defund the law of the land, "Obamacare."

Their entire party is built on resisting government. They've created this "boogeyman" called the Federal Government that they blame every problem in America on. Then their supporters, and a few of their politicians, advocate secession whenever they don't get their way. Some even talk of the violent overthrow of our government in an attempt to "take the country back." These irrational thoughts and rants are often the results of something not going their way.

This is the party that was once represented by the likes of Abraham Lincoln, Teddy Roosevelt and Dwight Eisenhower. They're now represented by people like Rand Paul, Ted Cruz and John Boehner. Talk about a massive drop-off in quality of representation.

A party that once had a president bring the country to civil war in the fight to free slaves, is now the one that will risk destroying it's economy to deny millions of Americans health care.

So please, tell me, how aren't Republicans a form of domestic terrorists? Isn't the basic premise for a terroristic act against the United States a deliberate act to harm Americans or American interests? As I said in the piece I wrote a few days ago, imagine if Islamic radicals were threatening to sink our nation's economy if they didn't get their way. Would we not call that a threat of terror?

Because that's the very threat Republicans are now using. Give into their demands or they'll harm millions of Americans and quite possibly crash our economy on purpose.

A main difference I see is that while al Qaeda might make threats to harm Americans and hurt our nation's economy, yet lack the ability to do either. Republicans are making those very same threats and seem poised to actually do both.

Has anyone noticed that on all United Nations treaties the same 4 groups all vote no. Fact, the only countries in the UN that currently vote no on all treaties are North Korea, Iran, Syria, and Republicans. The UN Treaty adopting our AMA law was defeated by the Republicans, now they are against the anti terrorist arms treaty. Both Treaties are current US laws and no changes to any law is actually required to be in compliance.

I swear these tin foil hat, afraid of the black helicopters, put us in FEMA camps and confiscate our guns wing nuts are insane, anti intellectual, anti diplomacy, our God is better than your God, shoot first and ask no questions Teanuckles really frost my onions. Doctors can grow a human brain in a lab, but no amount of science can grow a brain in a Conservative's head. The UN is a good thing. They try to stop wars and fight to protect human rights. It is a place where disputing Countries can try to negotiate peaceful outcomes. I can not understand why Conservatives and Republicans are universally against anything UN.

What the UN actually does

The UN has 4 main purposes;

To keep peace throughout the world

To develop friendly relations among nations

To help nations work together to improve the lives of poor people, to conquer hunger, disease and illiteracy, and to encourage respect for each others rights and freedoms

To be a center for harmonizing the actions of nations to achieve these goals.

They strive for the following agendas;

Maintaining Peace and Security
Making Peace
Preventing Nuclear Proliferation
Clearing Landmines
Combating Terrorism
Promoting Economic Development
Alleviating Rural Poverty in Developing Countries
Focusing on African Development
Promoting Woman's Well-being
Laying Groundwork for Business
Supporting Industry in Developing Countries
Fighting Hunger
Improving Global Trade Relations

Promoting Economic Reform through The
International Monetary Fund (IMF)   and   the
World Bank
Improving Aviation and Shipping
Generating Worldwide Commitment in Support of
Children through UNICEF
Turning Slums into Decent Human Settlements

A little something I put together for someone;

War is Terrorism
All War is Terrorism
The War on Terror is Terrorism
The War on Drugs is Terrorism
The War on Women is Terrorism
The War on Voters is Terrorism
The War on Minorities is Terrorism
We are Terrorists

Civil Rights

Do you know what the Southern Strategy is?

The "Southern Strategy" refers to the Republican Party's strategy of gaining political support or winning elections in the Southern United States by appealing to racism against African Americans. It began with Richard Nixon and Barry Goldwater in the late 1960s right after the African-American Civil Rights Movement, the passage of the Civil Rights Act of 1964, Voting Rights Act of 1965, and desegregation.

Bob Herbert, a New York Times columnist, wrote about the Southern Strategy in the early 1980s "The truth is that there was very little that was subconscious about the GOP's relentless appeal to racist whites. Tired of losing elections, it saw an opportunity to renew itself by opening it's arms wide to white voters who could never forgive the Democratic Party for it's support of civil rights and voting rights for blacks."

Which States exactly are considered the "Southern States"? the US Census Bureau defines them as; Delaware, Maryland, Virginia, West Virginia, Kentucky, North Carolina, South Carolina, Tennessee, Arkansas, Oklahoma, Texas, Louisiana, Mississippi, Alabama, Georgia, and Florida. The list includes all of the former

Confederate States, you could add Missouri, Kansas, New Mexico, and Arizona as they fall ideologically similar. Republicans have taken this strategy National, and use it in all States now.

When a candidate is for "States Rights" this is regarded as a "codeword" of opposition to federal enforcement of civil rights for blacks and intervention on their behalf, including passage of legislation.

After the death of Dr. Martin Luther King, some Black leaders called for action. There were riots and the idea of "Black Power" was born. Other incidents of Violence, Draft Card burning, Drugs, Free Love, and the Hippie counter culture, all of which came out of the Vietnam War protests created a new fear that could be harnessed and used. Republicans used this new fear of Blacks with a "codeword" term called "Law and Order" and was frequently used with "States Rights" as part of election platforms. According to the ACLU The War on Crime "disproportionately targets young men of color."

Other "Dog Whistle" or "Catch Phrase Code" issues include the terms "Affirmative Action" "Forced Busing", "Racial Quotas", "Food Stamps", and the more abstract "We Want To Cut this" when referring to "Social Safety Net" programs. "Being Ready" for public office is another code catch phrase. There are the more absurd such as "Welfare Queen", and "Buck". "Uppity" certainly.

Some "Jim Crow" Laws are; Racial Segregation, Black Codes, Poll Taxes, Literacy, Comprehension Tests, Residency, Record Keeping Requirements, Grandfather Clauses, and a variety of other Voter Suppression Laws strictly designed to disenfranchise Black and other Minority voters. This now includes the cutting of Early Voting, and Voter ID Laws. All of these things are illegal and unconstitutional according to the Civil Rights Act of 1964 and Voting Rights Act of 1965, we have seen legislation anyway by many Red States. The recent SCOTUS ruling striking down Article 4 of the Voting Rights Act has emboldened many Southern States to push Jim Crow legislation hard. Texas and North Carolina have passed some of the worst and most dangerous in our lifetime.

Black Poverty and a Lack of Education affects their ability to fight politically. The education system is funded by local communities, so the quality of education is a reflection of the economic level of each community. Low income communities can not afford the same quality education that higher income communities can. Another fact of education in low income communities is the apathy of both students and teachers. To them the children of the poor or ignorant are perceived as just copies of their parents, destined to live out the same poor old ignorant life. The effect of that perception are teachers that don't put in the effort to teach, and students that are not interested in learning, in both instances the idea is that the poor student is unable or incapable. Women in poverty are also likely to become pregnant at a younger age, and with fewer resources to take care of a child, girls often drop out of school. Due to these and other reasons the education between the classes and races is certainly not equal. This is all part and parcel of a mission creep to hold down poor and minority voters.

From 1981 to 1997, the United States Department of Agriculture discriminated against tens of thousands of Black American farmers, denying loans provided to white farmers in similar circumstances. This was designed to keep the Black rural community down. Period.

The "War on Drugs" was designed to be used as a racist political tool. If you are Black or a Minority living in a Southern State and the police catch you with even a small little bit of something illegal, say for instance, a marijuana joint, they prosecute you and convict you of a Felony. Once convicted, even if you only serve community service or parole. You lose your right to vote permanently. Bam, Instant and permanent Voter suppression. Where as if your white they do not prosecute you and/or your sentence is lowered to a Misdemeanor, no harm, no foul. When you look at the statistic that 75% of all Black males in Louisiana are convicted of a felony and fall into this category, then you understand why they use this this tactic.

Republicans have used the Southern Strategy against all minorities not just African Americans. They target Native American Indians, Indians, Latinos, Asians, Middle Eastern, Jewish, and "anyone who doesn't look like them", or is not "Christian", Muslims are a key focus currently. Recently they have also included women and the youth of America. Voter Suppression of College Campuses is an active legislative agenda. The blatant misogyny whether it is truly against all women or just aimed at poor and minority women is unclear. One fact remains, it is one of the GOP's highest agenda items in just the last few years with over 1000 bills and laws pushed through Congress as well as all of the "Red" States on Anti-abortion, Anti-contraception, Re-defining rape, etc...

Let me recapitulate all of this; The next time you hear any GOP candidate on any level say that he is "For States Rights and/or a Law and Order

Candidate, or that he wants to cut or eliminate any Social Spending, Food Stamps, or Welfare." Limit or drug test for any of these programs. A giant gong of a bell should go off in your head. This is Racism. This is the Southern Strategy.

Here is a partial list of Southern Strategy issues;
Voter ID laws
College Campus voter restrictions
Cutting of Early Voting days
Restricting new or early Voter registration
Eliminating Same Day Voter registration
Voter Purges
Redistricting or Gerrymandering
Cutting Welfare
Cutting Food Stamps (SNAP)
Cutting Unemployment Insurance
Cutting or Eliminating the Department of Education
Private School Vouchers
Attacks on Teachers and Teachers Unions
Cuts to Medicare and Medicaid
Defunding Planned Parenthood

In response to a post by my friend Chuck;
While Jim Crow laws were created by Democrats in the South, and yes they supported the KKK. I am afraid Chuck that you are being duped.

These Democrats were known as the Dixie-Crats and were extremely Conservative. It took a

Liberal Democrat to overturn these laws... His name was Lyndon B Johnson who signed into law the Civil Rights Act of 1964 and Voting Rights Act of 1965.

In defense of Margaret Sanger in a meme;
Margaret Sanger was in fact not racist, She was involved in the "Negro Project" which was organized to help provide birth control to African-American women. During the debate within the Birth Control Federation of America, which was sponsoring the project. Sanger argued very strongly that there should be African-American leadership in the Project. A single Sanger quote relating to this debate seems to be the basis for almost all the discussion on the internet of Sanger being racist: "we do not want word to go out that we want to exterminate the Negro population and the minister is the man who can straighten out that idea if it ever occurs to any of their more rebellious members." This has been interpreted by some people like Angela Davis) as proof that the project was actually a secret conspiracy to exterminate African-Americans. I find it a bit ironic that conservatives are, perhaps unwittingly, agreeing with Davis diagnosis of a white conspiracy. In fact, in the context of the debate Sanger was having with other members of the Birth Control Federation, the real meaning was almost certainly that she believed that black leadership was necessary to prevent the

mistaken belief that the purpose of the project was racist. In another quote from this debate Sanger stated: "I do not believe that this project should be directed or run by white medical men. The Federation should direct it with the guidance and assistance of the colored group..." Sanger herself said of the Negro Project, which was supported by prominent African-American civil rights activists like W.E.B. DuBois and Mary Bethune McLeod. that it was designed to help: "a group notoriously underprivileged and handicapped to a large measure by a 'caste' system that operates as an added weight upon their efforts to get a fair share of the better things in life. To give them the means of helping themselves is perhaps the richest gift of all. We believe birth control knowledge brought to this group, is the most direct, constructive aid that can be given them to improve their immediate situation."

Every quote from Sanger that I've been able to find suggests that she was in fact extremely sympathetic to the plight of minority groups like African-Americans.

Clarence Thomas was attacked by Liberals because he was Conservative. He was nominated to replace Thurgood Marshall who was the first African American Justice on the Supreme Court, The appointment of Thomas kept the existing racial makeup of the Court, But was likely to move the ideological needle to the right. Attorney General Richard Thornburgh warned Bush that replacing Marshall, who was revered as a civil rights movement icon, with any candidate who did not share Marshall's views would make the confirmation process difficult. Civil rights and feminist organizations opposed the Thomas appointment, because Thomas's was against affirmative action and because they felt that Thomas would not be a supporter of Roe v. Wade. Thomas had also been accused of Sexual harassment by Anita Hill who worked with Thomas at the DOJ.

With Regard to Bill Clinton, there was no harassment, Monica Lewinski was apparently a willing participant. So you are comparing apples and oranges.

The rest of the bullet points on your meme are simply Right wing talking points and are of no specific consequence.

How to fix the Civil Rights Act of 1964

Since the SCOTUS ruling striking down Article 4, we have seen all of the Southern States immediately begin to implement Voting Suppression legislation, basically bringing back "Jim Crow" laws.

All of this can be fixed quite easily, all Congress has to do is pass a Bill refitting Article 4 with no State exclusions.

"The Department of Justice must review and approve all State laws regarding voting, to verify that is does not impede any individual, sex, race, group, or demographic's ability to vote in their State."

That simple change would eliminate the SCOTUS argument of an unfair restriction of States Rights.

Write, Email, or Call your Racist Congressman Today and suggest this fix.

Minimum Wage

The best argument I could find for raising the minimum wage is Henry Ford who was an American industrialist, the founder of the Ford Motor Company, and Father of the assembly line technique of mass production. Although Ford did not invent the automobile, he developed and manufactured the first automobile that many middle class Americans could afford to buy. His introduction of the Model T automobile revolutionized transportation and American industry. As owner of the Ford Motor Company, he became one of the richest and best known people in the world. He is credited with "Fordism," mass production of inexpensive goods coupled with high wages for workers. Ford had a global vision, with consumerism as the key to peace. His commitment to lowering costs resulted in many technical and business innovations, including a franchise system that put dealerships throughout most of North America and in major cities on six continents.

Ford shocked the world in 1914 by offering a $5 per day wage, doubled the wage of most of his workers. A Cleveland, Ohio newspaper editorialized that the announcement "shot like a blinding rocket through the dark clouds of the present industrial depression." The move proved profitable. Instead of constant turnover of employees, the best mechanics in Detroit wanted to work for Ford, bringing their expertise, increasing productivity, and lowered training costs. Ford announced his $5 per day program in January 1914, raising the minimum daily pay from $2.34 to $5 for most workers. It also set a new, reduced work week, although the details vary in different accounts. Ford in 1922 said it was "six 8 hour days, giving a 48-hour week", later in 1926 he described it as "five 8 hour days, giving a 40-hour week". The program started with Saturdays as workdays and then later it was changed to a second day off.

Detroit was already a high wage city, but competitors were forced to raise wages or lose their best workers. Ford's policy proved, however, that paying people more would enable Ford workers to afford the cars they were producing and be good for the economy. Ford explained the policy as profit sharing rather than wages.

Using this proven example we should do more than increase minimum wage to $9, we should consider what Switzerland just did and raise our minimum wage much, much more. The Swiss raised theirs to $50,000 per year, while at the same time they put restrictions on executives and CEO pay and bonuses.

Trickle Up Economics Begins

For decades now we have heard over and over again about "Trickle Down" economics. It has been a complete failure, a lie, a canard, right wing bull crap. Originally brought onto the US political scene by Ronald Reagan. Trickle down has been nothing but a way to make the rich richer and the poor poorer. It is the mainstay of income inequality in America.

Now new thinking must replace this failed policy. It is pretty much the exact opposite, let's call it Trickle Up economics. The premise being that if you give more money to the working poor and the middle class it will have a much more stimulative effect on the economy because any additional money that these classes of people receive they will almost immediately spend.

If the poor and part time workers earn more they will not have to rely so much on government programs like welfare or food stamps. Corporation's profit's are at all time historical highs, never have they made more in history, paying workers more seems like a natural step. Getting corporations to increase wages is harder than pulling teeth. These greedy bastards never let any money actually "trickle down". They never have, and they all never will, unless they are actually forced to. That is a fact, a sad, but true one. CEOs give them selves huge multimillion dollar raises each and every year, pay top executives ginormous salaries. Yet year after year we hear the same old tired excuses. Pay freezes, 1% raises, austerity till the economy improves, costs have gone up. Any and every reason to pay lower end employees as little as possible. Fair wages are harder and harder to find.

That paradigm is about to go the way of the Dodo bird. The concept of a living wage has found it's way into America. Washington State is the home of Seattle-Tacoma International Airport, which employs over 6,000 workers. Most of the jobs there are lower rung, many are baggage handlers, jet fuelers, maintenance workers, and cabin cleaners. They often rely on food stamps to feed their families, which frees up what little they earn for bills and rent. Sea-Tac shares the same income inequality problems as the rest of the country. 31% of their children live in poverty. The cost of living in the region is high, making ends meet is difficult especially in the poorer neighborhoods. So the people of Sea-Tac decided they had had enough, and put an airport workers minimum wage initiative on the ballot, which won approval in the latest election.

Proposition 1 gives Sea-Tac employees a $15.00 minimum wage, allows them to keep their tips, and provides for paid sick days. These are benefit's many higher-wage and salaried workers take for granted, but are incredibly rare for lower income employees. This is the kind of "Trickle Up" stimulus the local economy needs . The kind of Trickle up stimulus the whole country needs. More money earned means more to spend, more to save, and no need for Government programs. A ripple up effect begins there, one study estimated that $54 million in economic activity will stimulate new jobs and growth, increasing the Sea-Tac region's workforce. This is exactly what we need, exactly what the people of Sea-Tac need, exactly what America needs. We need to shine a very bright light on this, expose it to the scrutiny of sunlight even. As more and more people see how this policy will benefit all of us and expose the darkness of the lie that was Trickle down.

Americans need ever increasing income and not stagnant wages and salaries., Simply much better opportunities. The middle class of America needs to be re-energized, re-structured, re-built, with an inflow of money. it needs to start at the very bottom, with an actual living minimum wage. Thank you people of Sea-Tac, thank you for bringing this so important living wage issue to the ballot box. This is a ray of hope that democracy can serve the people and not the heinous corporations who have oppressed us.

Recently we have seen efforts across the US try either try or succeed in raising their minimum wage. New Jersey in fact did over ride Governor Christie's veto and raised their states minimum wage to $8.25 per hour. Massachusetts is in the process to raise theirs to $11, the fight continues. The Senate has promised to bring forth a national raise, we shall see. Trickle up economics, according to Keynes, at least has a chance of working, unlike that trickle down nonsense.

The Poor

Facts about Food Stamps or SNAP;

20% of US Households sometimes do not have enough to feed their Children.

SNAP only gives people enough for 21 meals per Month

Who is Eligible to Receive SNAP benefit's?

Households of 4 with less than $2000 in assets.

Households of 4 with less than $1,767 in Monthly income.

Able bodied applicants must meet work requirements.

What is Eligible for Purchase with SNAP benefit's?
Bread, cereal, fruit's, vegetables, meat, fish, poultry, and dairy products.

Seeds and plants which produce food to eat.

You CANNOT use SNAP benefit's to buy
Beer, Wine, Liquor, Cigarettes, Tobacco, Vitamins, Medicines, Diapers and Tampons.

Food that will be eaten in the store or Hot foods.

Characteristics of SNAP households?

50% are Children.

29% are Elderly or Disabled.

87% of households include Children, Elderly, or the Disabled.

Over 900,000 Veteran's households receive SNAP.

63% are White and 38% are Native American.

Fraud?

According to the USDA in 2012 there were 342 Convictions and $58 Million in abuses. That comes out to LESS THAN 1%. Conservative claims all of those Welfare Queens and abuses like buying Lobster Amounts to only 1% of the entire program.

If you still believe that we should cut Food Stamp Funding. Please Shut up Now, you have no idea what your talking about.

Immigration

Think about it this way for a second. Suppose you went to another Country, we shall call it Itsnotsobad. Most Likely you would be in an area where the locals speak both English and Itzish. Signs are in both languages as well. Your Cousins who live there speak Itzish, as well as English. When you have to fill out forms they are available in both languages. Then you find out that Itsnotsobad doesn't have an official language and they provide forms and signs in almost all major languages. There is no legal reason or compulsion to learn Itzish. Would you spend money that you don't have to take Itzish classes? Would you get a book and try to teach Itzish to yourself? Just asking the questions here to play a little devils advocate.

Currently in the US there is absolutely not a single legal word written in the Constitution, the Amendments, in any State Statute, actually not in any legal brief, file, or writ. Theoretically we could make the official language anything we wanted even Itzish. I guess what I am saying is if you really feel that strongly that any visitor or immigrant learn English mandatory, maybe there ought to at least be a law first?

Another well used argument is that our parents and grandparents had to learn English, so they should as well. I counter that argument with the fact that when our fore people came to the US they were accepted in without any pre conditions other than communicable disease and violent felony convictions. All were encouraged to become US Citizens and there were no restrictive fees. Currently it costs on average $8,000 to $10,000 per person in legal fees and the waiting period may be as long as 20 years. This makes "Legal" immigration impossible. Again, if the shoe was on your foot, and you could not move to Itsnotsobad legally and be allowed to become an Itsnotsobad citizen, what incentive would you have to learn Itzish?

Steve, (responding to a friend of mine) you mentioned your time when in South Korea. They do have an official language which is Korean.

According to the 2010 Census almost 20% of us speak other languages including Spanish, French, Italian, Portuguese, German, Yiddish, Swedish, Danish, Greek, Russian, Polish, in Total over 350 different languages. So not all of us speak English.

In Europe most people speak at least two languages and sometimes many more. Speaking multiple languages is considered basic education in most other Countries. In the grand scheme of things, is it really such an inconvenience to have to press 1 extra button for a phone call to go through? Surely there are more important issues to debate and complain about, perhaps immigration reform? He he...

I simply don't recognize America anymore. As a child growing up I was taught that America is a virtual melting pot of immigrants. That our diversity was one of our great strengths. I was told stories of how everyone's grandparents or great grandparents all came to America seeking a better life and place for their children. We have all heard the stories of people coming here and seeing the stature of liberty for the first time and being processed through Ellis island. How last names got changed, or misspelled. How so many of those immigrants became US citizens and so many served in the military, started businesses, bought houses. This was our true American way. The only ones denied entry were hardcore criminals and any people with communicable diseases. Entry was free, all were encouraged to become citizens. Where and how did we go so wrong?

Currently there does not seem to even be a way for the modern immigrant to enter legally. So many roadblocks have been put up to stop anyone from entry. Cost run into the thousands of dollars per person. Waiting periods run into the decades. I say swing wide open the gates of freedom once again. Robust immigration will stimulate the economy, as well as the housing market. Small businesses will once again thrive and grow. The tax base will be expanded as well as revenue. Immigration strengthens us in so many ways. How the heck is it possible that a Country of immigrants, Irish, Scottish, British, Italian, German, Japanese, Chinese, Russian, Ukrainian, Hungarian, etc... Can possibly now be against the same opportunity as our own families were afforded? This is nonsense of the first magnitude. Who we now call "Illegal Immigrants" would have all been considered legal just a few years ago. Right the injustice, allow a path to citizenship, allow immigration the way it was for the first 200 years of our history. We must refrain from the prejudice we now have toward these foreigners who want nothing more than an opportunity and a better life for their children. If we wind up with a few bad apples in the mix, so be it. The benefit's of the many out weigh the needs of the few. Do not give in to fear and loathing of the unknown, rather embrace our legacy of freedom.

US border security; There are 2,069 miles of East Coast Shoreline, 1,631 miles of Gulf Coast shoreline, 7,623 miles of pacific shoreline, 1,060 miles of Alaska/Arctic shoreline, and 5,525 miles of US Canadian border. Can anyone actually explain to me or to all of us why Conservatives and Republicans aren't screaming bloody freaking murder about building a giant electrified fence up along all of those borders?

Abortion

If you believe that Abortion should be illegal, you are in the Minority! The Majority of Americans are in favor of Legal Abortion.

Here is the results from all of the current polls;

July 2013 Quinnipiac University Poll

"Do you think abortion should be legal in all cases, legal in most cases, illegal in most cases or illegal in all cases?"

Legal in all cases - 58%
Legal in most cases - 20%
Illegal in most cases - 25%
Illegal in all cases - 12%
Unsure/No answer - 5%
Total For Legal Abortion was 58%

"The U.S. Supreme Court has said abortion is legal without restriction in about the first 24 weeks of pregnancy. Some states have passed laws reducing this to 20 weeks. If it has to be one or the other, would you rather have abortions

Legal without restriction up to 20 weeks, or up to 24 weeks?"

Up to 20 weeks – 55%

Up to 24 weeks – 30%
Never legal - 7%
Always legal – 1%
Unsure/No answer - 7%
Total For Legal Abortion was 86%

July 2013   CBS News Poll

"Which of these comes closest to your view?
Abortion should be generally available to those
who want it. OR, Abortion should be available,
but under stricter limit's than it is now. OR,
Abortion should not be permitted."

Generally available - 37%
Available under stricter limit's - 40%
Not permitted - 21%
Unsure - 2%
Total For Legal Abortion was 77%

May 2013 CNN / ORC Poll

"Do you think abortion should be legal under any
circumstances, legal only under certain
circumstances, or illegal in all circumstances?"

Always legal - 25%
Sometimes legal - 54%
Always illegal - 20%
Unsure - 1%
Total for Legal Abortion was 79%

"Do you think abortion should be legal under any circumstances, legal under only certain circumstances, or illegal in all circumstances?" If "legal under only certain circumstances": "Do you think abortion should be legal in most circumstances or only a few circumstances?"

Always legal - 25%
Legal in most Circumstances - 11%
Always illegal - 20%
Unsure - 1%
Total for Legal Abortion was 78%

May 2013 Gallup Poll

"Do you think abortions should be legal under any circumstances, legal only under certain circumstances, or illegal in all circumstances?"

Always legal - 26%
Sometimes legal - 52%
Always illegal - 20%
Unsure - 2%
Total for Legal Abortion was 78%

Shouldn't the Law of the Land be what the Majority of the American people want?

Keep your Religion out of our Politics!
Keep your Religion out of our Government!
Keep your Religion out of our Constitution!

Some Abortion facts;

The US abortion rate fell 29% between 1990 and 2005, from 27.4 to 19.4 abortions per 1,000 women of childbearing age, before leveling out from 2005-2008.

An abortion can cost anywhere from around $350 to more than $1,000. In 2009, it was estimated that a total of $831 million is spent on abortions annually.

Back alley or illegal abortions cause 68,000 maternal deaths each year in the 33 countries where abortion is not legal or available, according to the World Health Organization in Oct. 2006.

Black women are 4.5 times as likely as white women to have an abortion, and about 1,876 black fetuses are aborted every day.

87% of US Counties do not provide abortion services.

Here is a list of Pro Choice arguments;

A woman's right to choose to have an abortion is a "Fundamental Right" recognized as such by the US Supreme Court. The landmark abortion case Roe v. Wade was decided on Jan 22, 1973, and remains till Today as the law of the land.

Personhood begins at birth, and first breath, not at conception. Abortion is the termination of a pregnancy and not a child. Personhood at conception is not a proven biological fact. Many religions believe personhood and a soul begins with the child's first breath.

Fetuses are incapable and do not feel pain when an abortion is performed. According to Stuart WG Derbyshire, PhD, Senior Lecturer at the University of Birmingham, England, "Not only has the biological development not yet occurred to support pain experience, but the environment after birth, so necessary to the development of pain experience, is also yet to occur."

Access to legal, professionally performed abortions reduces injury and death caused by unsafe, illegal abortions. The World Health Organization estimated in 2006 that "Back Alley" abortions cause 68,000 maternal deaths each year in countries where abortion is not legal.

The anti abortion or pro life position is solely based on religion only, and threatens the First Amendment ideal of separation of church and state. Religious ideology should not be now, or ever, a foundation or base for law in the United States. Christian law, like Sharia law, is forbidden.

Modern abortion procedures are safe. The risk of a woman's death from abortion is less than one in 100,000 whereas the risk of a woman dying from giving birth is 13.3 deaths per 100,000 pregnancies. Furthermore, a 1993 fertility investigation of 10,767 women by the Joint Royal College of General Practitioners and Royal College of Obstetricians and Gynecologists found that women who had at least two abortions experienced the same future fertility as those who had at least two natural pregnancies.

Access to abortion is absolutely 100% necessary because contraceptives are not always available. Women need a doctor's prescription to obtain many types of birth control, like the pill, the patch, the shot, and the diaphragm. Half of all group insurance plans do not cover any form of prescription contraception, and only a third cover the pill. A July/Aug 2001 Guttmacher Institute study of health care insurers found that "75% of insured women lacked coverage for contraceptive services. As of 2009, 17 million US women were completely uninsured." Of note is that the American Care Act or Obamacare corrects this injustice.

The American Medical Association or AMA, recognizes abortion as a legitimate medical procedure when performed by a licensed doctor and done with good medical practice standards.

There are over 1,800 licensed doctors who provide abortions in the US. These doctors, the actual patient, and not moron politicians, should have the authority to make medical decisions about abortion.

Abortion gives couples the option to choose not to bring babies with severe and life-threatening medical conditions to full term. Fragile X syndrome, the most common genetic form of mental retardation, affects about 1 in 4,000 males and 1 in 8,000 females. One in 800 babies have Down Syndrome, and one in 3,500 babies are born with Cystic Fibrosis. It is wrong to sentence a child to life with an acute handicap. Keep in mind if this goes against your personal beliefs you may do as you wish. We have freedom of religion here remember?

Many women who choose to have an abortion don't have the financial means to support a child. A September 2005 survey done by the journal "Perspectives on Sexual and Reproductive Health" asked women "Why they had an abortion"? said that 73% of respondents said "They could not afford to have a baby", and 38% said "Giving birth would interfere with their education and career goals". Reproductive choice helps protect women from some financial disadvantage.

Motherhood must never be a punishment for having sexual intercourse. President Barack Obama said during a Mar. 29, 2008 campaign speech in Johnston, Pennsylvania, "I have two daughters... I'm going to teach them first about values and morals, but if they make a mistake, I don't want them punished with a baby."

A baby should not come into the world unwanted. 49% of all pregnancies among American women are unintended. Having a child is an important lifelong decision that requires consideration, preparation, and planning.

Abortion is good tool for population control. Malnutrition, starvation, poverty, lack of medical and educational services, pollution, under development, and conflicts over resources are all serious consequences of over population.

Any links between abortion procedures and getting breast cancer is simply just not true. The National Cancer Institute (NCI), the American Cancer Society (ACS), and the American College of Obstetricians and Gynecologists (ACOG) have all refuted multiple studies claiming having an abortion leads directly to a higher percentage of getting breast cancer.

Abortion reduces crime. Some estimates claim legalized abortion accounted for as much as 50%

of the drop in murder, property crime, and violent crime between 1973 and 2001. Teenage girls, unmarried women, and poor women are more likely to have unintended pregnancies, and since unwanted babies are often raised in poverty, their chances of leading criminal lives in adulthood are increased.

While debates and discussions rage around this issue, the only correct and factual answer is that legal abortion is the law of the land in the US and the decision is the right of each woman when looked at through the lens of civil reason. All women have the right to choose, not choose, as their personal beliefs and feelings move them. This is a civil matter that should never even be discussed politically. It is a religious issue only and should remain such. Especially since the United States is a Secular nation that has a distinct separation of church and state through the first amendment of the US Constitution.

In conclusion if you believe that it is morally wrong to have an abortion, then don't get one. That is your choice. Not the Governments. End of discussion.

Gun Control

Amendment II to the US Constitution;
"A well regulated Militia, being necessary to the security of a free State, the right of the people to keep and bear Arms, shall not be infringed".

Americans just love their guns. People from both political parties agree with the second amendment and pretty much both support it. There in lies the rub, no single party, not even the Democrats are willing to take this issue head on. In fact even I own firearms and believe in the Second Amendment. I do however believe that as in all things government, common sense regulations are required.

There certainly should be political wiggle room for some gun control. Lets be brutally honest without regulation what would stop people from buying and owning nuclear missiles? Giant Howitzers, Tanks, battleships, hand grenades, etc... Obviously the question becomes where to draw the lines, rather than no lines at all.

Here are some facts in regard to gun control.

More Guns Equals More Homicides, There is a direct line correlation between gun ownership and homicides. This according to data from the Harvard School of Public Health.

More Guns Equals More Suicides, People who own guns have a suicide rate double those that do not. The Boston Globe did a report on this, but many others also agree. suicide is not so much a rational decision, but something people do on the spur of the moment. Access to a gun increases follow though.

Americans want some gun control,here are some stark facts compiled from numerous polls;

40% of all US homes have guns.

81% of Americans say gun control is an important issue in determining which candidates to vote for.

91% of Americans say that there should be at least some restrictions on gun ownership.

Between 57% and 95% are for various issues like bans on high capacity magazines, assault rifles, Large caliber bullets, etc... Vary from issue to issue. These numbers cross party lines and most are supported even by NRA members.

57% of Americans say that there should be major restrictions or a ban.

Child Safety Locks issue, In 1996, 140 children died after being accidentally shot. About 1,500 children are hurt by guns every year. "Trigger Locks" require entering a combination to use the gun, or some other locking method. they are intended to reduce inadvertent use by children or other unauthorized users.

Background Checks, The "Gun Show Loophole" means that there are no background checks when purchasing guns in a private transaction. Guns sold at gun shows through dealers are subject to background checks, only those sold privately are not.

Right to Bear Arms, The Supreme Court ruled in 1939, in a case US v. Miller, that the second amendment only protects guns suitable for a well regulated militia. example, "sawed off" shotguns can be banned because they're not "ordinary military equipment."

Since 1939, the Supreme Court has not heard any other, or additional second amendment cases. The most recent ruling before the "Heller" ruling, in 1997, overturned part of the 1993 Brady Bill. But it did not address second amendment rights. "Heller" refers to a ruling on the issue of individual rights. The Supreme Court ruled, in the 2008 case District of Columbia v. Heller, that the second Amendment does define an "individual right" to gun ownership, as opposed to a "collective right" for a "state run and state armed

National Guard". Much discretion was left to the states and to Congress, but Heller opens up the issue to further Supreme Court cases. So, gun control issues are still primarily under the control of Congress.

Discussions about gun control very often focus on the Washington DC handgun ban because uniquely Congress has direct control of those laws within the District of Columbia. One of those laws was at issue in the Heller case.

Gun Control Buzz words to listen and watch out for. The biggest part of the Gun Control discussion is whether existing gun laws are enough, or more laws are needed.

Liberals and populists generally favor more gun laws. Look for buzz words like "more registration" or "more licensing" to describe seeking further restrictions legal ownership; or "close the loopholes" and "restrict access" for further restrictions on illegal ownership. Moderate liberals and populists will generally favor more restrictions on ownership while paying lip service "Sportsmen's rights" or respecting "the right of self-protection." A moderate compromise is to "extend waiting periods" before allowing ownership, to perform "background checks" of varying degrees of severity.

Conservatives and libertarians generally oppose gun laws. Look for buzz words like "Second Amendment Rights" or "allow concealed carry." A call for "instant background checks" pays lip service to gun control advocates as it sounds like a restriction, but means allowing purchasing guns on the spot.

Moderate conservatives and libertarians oppose gun laws while acknowledging that restrictions are inevitable. Look for buzz words like "enforce existing gun laws," which implies not passing any new gun laws. Similarly, "more strict enforcement" of gun laws implies a pro gun rights stance, unless it is accompanied by a call for new gun laws.

Centrists and moderates from both the right and left generally support restrictions on juvenile access to guns, especially in the wake of tragedies like Littleton and other gun related deaths.

Positive mentions of the NRA, the National Rifle Association, the largest pro-gun rights lobbying group, implies support of gun rights, while opposing the NRA or "taking on the gun lobby" implies support of gun restrictions.

Multiple states now have "Stand Your Ground" laws, which justify the use of deadly force when "threatened", as opposed to the older legal principle of an "obligation to retreat" first. The Florida version of the "stand your ground" law gained national attention in February 2012 with the Trayvon Martin shooting. Martin, an unarmed black teenager, was shot and killed by a "neighborhood watch" coordinator, George Zimmerman. Citing the "stand your ground" law, Zimmerman was not initially charged, but was later arrested. Zimmerman was later acquitted.

"Stand Your Ground" laws are whats known as model legislation that was put together by ALEC and the NRA. Many believe, as do I, that this idea was created to "fix" a non existent problem. Laws like this are politically activist much like the "Voter ID" laws, useless and not needed for any actual reason. Stand your ground has one purpose which is to sell more guns. Period.

Here is a rather interesting fact, In the 1930s, because of gun violence by organized crime during Prohibition, the National Firearms Act and the Federal Firearms Act were both written and passed, banning true machine guns. When was the last time you heard or read about a mass shooting with a machine gun? There has not been one actual incident since.

So we could extrapolate a direct correlation to banning specific weapons and their use in tragic shootings. The last word on this is if over 92% of Americans want something to become a law, then it should become law. Isn't that how a democracy works?

At last check over 92% of Americans including 75% of National Rifle Association members were for universal background checks.

Why is it then that only 8% of Americans don't want gun controls of any kind. Yet they have the NRA, a powerful industry and lobby group that can sway congress to their way of thinking? This is nonsense. You can tell your congressman that next election by voting... Last time I checked the People still have the power to make change in this Country.

The Tea Party

If you have to invoke Hitler and the Nazis in your argument. You lose the argument. Plain and simple. Ted Cruz called his own republicans Nazi appeasers. The Tea Party constantly references Hitler and Nazism when speaking about Obamacare and/or any of the Presidents policies. If you have to resort to such visceral garbage to make your point nobody will take you seriously. Pretty much immediately a major majority will discount what you have to say as worthless or nonsense. Anyone who is old enough to remember, or anyone who ever read a history book in school knows full well the difference between Nazi Fascism and Democratic or Republican policy. Words and visuals of this nature only show ignorance, bigotry and hatred. Nothing more. This is a third grade argument made by a child. Seriously if you have an objection to a current or proposed policy use facts and logic to make your point not scary images of long dead bad guys. Playground fear mongering is used by bully's for no good reason. This new "Overpass" group and the Tea Party ground crew are nothing more than children screaming about things they do not understand and using words they do not know the meaning of. These are the slow kids that failed math, science, and history and grew up ignorant. They bullied us in grade school, do not let them bully you now.

It's Deja Vu all over again. A quick synopsis of the 2012 election regarding Tea Party candidates. Just a few quick substitutions and we are right back to the 2008 elections. Standard Republican candidate swap out.

In the mainstream winner category, Mitt Romney was swapped for John McCain.

In the crazy Jesus guy category, Rick Santorum swapped for Mike Huckabee.

In the Divorced Wacko category, Rudy Giuliani Swapped for Newt Gingrich.

In the Conservative wing nut division, Fred Thompson Swapped for Rick Perry.

Ron Paul swapped for Ron Paul? OK, same guy still lunatic fringe.

The question I want answered is since the great "Tea Party" revolution in this country where is the great "Tea Party" candidate... Oh... That's right... I forgot, the Tea Party doesn't really exist. It was just a made up thing by the Republicans. And of course is completely and utterly irrelevant. All they did was trick you into voting Republican and of course to give them money. Ha Ha The jokes on you. Now your all stuck with the Party backed huckster Mitt Romney, the Father of President Obama's health care reform. A dyed in the wool "Good Old Rich Guy" who will sell your sorry asses down the river like he did to all those people who's companies he bought, shut down, laid off, and sent their jobs to China. It reminds me of a "Who" song... Meet the new boss, same as the old boss... Hope we don't get fooled again...

Extremists

Republicans are now a small band of brothers connected by a single mind of narrow thinking. They have made every effort to remove all trace of Liberal and Moderate members. They are a party of ideologues and religious fringe held together by a hatred of President Obama. Upon every political loss in elections they believe that more purity, more to the right, more conservatism is the answer. Their own studies have shown that they need to widen their appeal, the single issue that their report points to is immigration reform. So the current talking point is how they have to do immigration reform, they are for immigration reform, they want immigration reform, they are supposedly all about immigration reform, but now their actions betray them. The Senate, with the help of a number of Republicans have passed an immigration reform bill, the House will not even look at it, consider a vote on it, and have no reason to do a damn thing about it. Ha ha the joke is on them. While this is the single best issue to appeal to the Latino demographic, they simply can not get past their own bigotry to actually do anything other than leave the status quo. They can not compromise even with themselves. Anyone who steps even a little out of line on any issue is immediately threatened with a primary against them.

Rather than bi-partisan legislation on anything they have retreated to an against everything group, clinging to their religion and guns. Republicans turned to nasty personal attacks against President Obama, his healthcare legislation, his character, his childhood, where he was born, his religion, etc... A childish barrage of school yard bullying. They have pointed their crooked little fingers at every problem with the country and the economy, even on issues that happened before he was President. It is insane the disrespect they have hurled at the office of the President. Especially the House of Representatives leadership. Majority Leader Eric Cantor, Majority Whip Kevin McCarthy and Chairman of the House Budget Committee Paul Ryan.

Calling themselves the Young Guns, they made no bones about their misgivings of the new speaker of the House, John Boehner. They along with a base of about 70 Tea Party congressmen have set to obstruct and block any and everything unless they get their way. In fact this years 2013 House has so far passed not a single solitary bill of any significance greater than naming a new post office. Even the "Do Nothing" Congress of FD Roosevelt's era actually did more.
Here is a list of some of the more well known and influential "Tea Party" Extremists or as I like to

call them "Wing Nuts" and some of the highlights of their meaningless existence;

Michelle Bachman (R-MN)
She chairs the Tea Party Caucus in the House, and what a Whackadoo she is. The "Queen of the Tea Party" She reigns supreme with her iron fist, spouting literally insane theories about Muslim extremists infiltrating our government. Religious right anthems of pro life, anti abortion, anti contraceptives, anti LGBT anything. Calling for a Constitutional amendment to block marriage equality. Another Amendment to block the use of foreign currency in the US. She is an avid climate change denier. Made up the Obamacare Death Panels scare, and has called for the repeal of Obamacare at every opportunity. Wants to repeal Dodd-Frank entirely, opposes the minimum wage, no, not increases, the whole idea of it. Bachman has called for phasing out Social Security and Medicare entirely. Pretty much wants to nuke Iran. She is against the Dream act and any immigration. She constantly votes to cut welfare and food stamps all the while her family makes millions off of government subsidies. She is currently on the House intelligence committee, which actually makes me want to vomit. She is also under investigation for election finance fraud for using campaign money for personal use and not paying her campaign workers.

Actual things that Michelle Bachman has said;

"This health care reform cannot pass...What we have to do today is make a covenant, to slit our wrists, be blood brothers on this thing. This will not pass."

"The big thing we are working on now is the global warming hoax. It's all voodoo, nonsense, hokum, a hoax"

"What I would say, what I would say is that the news media should do a penetrating expose and take a look. I wish they would. I wish the American media would take a great look at the views of the people in Congress and find out, are they pro-America or anti-America? I think people would love to see an expose like that."

"This taxation is slavery, it's nothing more than slavery. The Constitution provides freedom."

"Last Friday a couple from Hawaii decided the time was so short they needed to get on a plane, come to Washington, to beg their representative to vote no, from Hawaii. What sacrifices freedom loving Americans are making to get their government's attention. And how big our government has gotten. They brought me this beautiful, precious lei and I'm reminded that the one who created this lei also created our freedom. "

"We're $14 trillion in debt, but that doesn't include the unfunded massive liabilities. That's $107 trillion, and that's for Social Security and Medicare and all the rest. You add up all those unfunded net liabilities, and all the traps that could go wrong we're on the hook for, and what it means is what we have to do is a reorganization of all of that, Social Security and all... But basically what we have to do is wean everybody else off. And wean everybody off because we have to take those unfunded net liabilities off our bank sheet, we can't do it. So we just have to be straight with people. So basically, whoever our nominee is, is going to have to have a Glenn Beck chalkboard and explain to everybody this is the way it is."

"But parents are going to excluded from Planned Parenthood as they write these clinics because the bill orders that these clinics protect patient privacy and student records. What does that mean? It means that parents will never know what kind of counsel and treatment that their children are receiving. And as a matter of fact, the bill goes on to say what's going to go on -- comprehensive primary health services, physicals, treatment of minor acute medical conditions, referrals to follow-up for specialty care -- is that abortion? Does that mean that someone's 13 year-old daughter could walk into a sex clinic, have a pregnancy test done, be taken away to the local Planned Parenthood abortion clinic, have their abortion, be back and go home on the school bus that night? Mom and dad are never the wiser."

Response to President Obama's 2011 State of the Union address: "The perilous battle that was fought during World War II in the Pacific at Iwo Jima was a battle against all odds, and yet this picture the iconic flag raising immortalizes the victory of young GIs over the incursion against the Japanese."

"I don't know how much God has to do to get the attention of the politicians. We've had an earthquake; we've had a hurricane. He said, 'Are you going to start listening to me here?'

"I haven't had a gaffe or something that I've done that has caused me to fall in the polls."

"I think what you're advocating for is censorship on the part of government. So the government would prohibit intelligent design from even the possibility of being taught in questioning the issue of evolution. And if you look at scientists there is not a unanimity of agreement on the origins of life. ... Why would we stall any particular theory? Because I don't think that even evolutionists, by and large, would say that this is proven fact. They say that this is a theory, as well as intelligent design. So I think the best thing to do is to let all scientific facts on the table, and let students decide.

"Carbon dioxide is natural, it is not harmful, it is a part of Earth's life cycle. And yet we're being told that we have to reduce this natural substance, reduce the American standard of living, to create an arbitrary reduction in something that is naturally occurring in Earth."

"We have to recognize that 15 of the sites, nuclear sites, are available or are potentially penetrable by Jihadists. Six attempts have already been made on nuclear sites. This is more than an existential threat...At this point, I would continue that aid. Pakistan is a nation that it's kind of like, too nuclear to fail."

"He has a perpetual magic wand and nobody's given him a spanking yet and taken it out of his hand." NOTE: this was a comment about President Obama and immigration reform.

"We have checked Michele Bachmann 13 times, and seven of her claims have been found to be false and six have been found to be ridiculously false... She is unusual in that regard that she has never gotten a rating higher than false"... Bill Adair, PolitiFact.com

"Michele Bachmann is a religious zealot whose brain is a raging electrical storm of divine visions and paranoid delusions... Bachmann is exactly the right kind of completely batshit crazy... crazy in the sense that she's living completely inside her own mind, frenetically pacing the hallways of a vast sand castle she's built in there, unable to meaningfully communicate with the human beings on the other side of the moat, who are all presumed to be enemies"... Matt Taibbi

Ted Cruz (R-TX)
Maverick Republican John McCain called Ted Cruz a "Wacko Bird". Ted Cruz is pro life and pro guns. He has threatened to filibuster any bills that are brought up on any of those issues. Last summer he did a nationwide tour to promote the repeal of Obamacare. He did a fake filibuster on the floor of the Senate promising to shut the government down if Obamacare was not repealed he then voted yes to pass the bill he just spoke against. Wait ? What? Holy smokes, really? Of note during that fake filibuster was when he recited Dr Seuss book Green Eggs and Ham. Of course the moral of that story was about someone who tried something then actually liked it. Doh. Current Senate Republican leader Mitch McConnell said this about Cruz's actions "not a smart play" and a "tactical error"

During the government shutdown and

negotiations over the debt ceiling Cruz held meetings with the Houses members, remember he is in the other Chamber. Without the Majority whips knowledge urging them to do it, go over the limit because their would be "No detrimental fallout".

Actual things that Ted Cruz has said;

On Obama's plot to kidnap him: "So this afternoon President Obama has invited the Senate Republicans to the White House. So after leaving here, I'm going to be going to the White House. I will make a request. if I'm never seen again, please send a search and rescue team. I very much hope by tomorrow morning I don't wake up amidst the Syrian rebels."

On the press: "The media wants America to give up and allow this country to keep sliding off the edge of the cliff."

On the Constitution: "This is an administration that seems bound and determine to violate every single one of our bill of rights. I don't know that they have yet violated the Third Amendment, but I expect them to start quartering soldiers in peoples' homes soon."

On the hecklers who interrupted his speech: "Is anybody left at OFA headquarters? I'm actually glad that the president's whole political staff is here instead of actually doing mischief in the country

On hecklers, again: "It would seem that President Obama's paid political operatives are out in force. The men and women in this room scare the living daylights out of them."

On hecklers, a third time: "How scared is the President? What a statement of fear, what a statement of fear. Oh, they don't want the truth to be heard. They definitely don't want the truth to be heard."

On the Cold War: "Our foreign policy is detente, which I'm pretty sure is French for surrender."

On Vice President Biden: "You don't need a punchline. You just say his name, people laugh."

By the way Ted Cruz father Raphael is even more outspoken and extreme right than his son appears

Rand Paul (R-KY)
When his Board Certification in Ophthalmology expired rather than re certifying he and 200 others formed their own "Board" so they can continue to say they are Board Certified, he is most certainly not, or at least not anymore. He

voted against a government funding bill twice. Helped filibuster and block President Obama nominations. Paul considers himself a Libertarian, 100% pro life meaning against abortion in every and all instances. Opposes any and all LGBT issue. Typically supports all of the usual Tea Party issues.

In an interview on the Rachel Maddow show he said that he "would not have voted for the civil Right Act of 1964".

His ghost writer had to step down when it was revealed that he was a staunch secessionist and Confederate sympathizer. Celebrating John Wilkes Booths birthday and all things Southern racist.

He has been outed by the press as a known serial plagiarist and rather than admitting any wrong doing actually displayed anger and "wished he could challenge the accusers to a pistol duel".

Actual things that Rand Paul has said;
"I think it's irresponsible of the president and his men to even talk about default. There's no reason for us to default. We bring in $250 billion in taxes every month. Our interest payment is $20 billion. Tell me why we would ever default. We have legislation called the Full Faith and

Credit Act, and it tells the president you must pay the interest on the debt. So this is a game."

"It's been in news reports that ships have been leaving from Libya and that they may have weapons and what I'd like to know is the annex that was close by, were they involved with procuring, buying, selling, obtaining weapons and were any of these weapons being transferred to other countries, any countries, Turkey included?"

"The size of growth of government is enormous under President Obama." - A known lie.

"Just because a couple people on the Supreme Court declare something to be 'constitutional' does not make it so. The whole thing remains unconstitutional. While the court may have erroneously come to the conclusion that the law is allowable, it certainly does nothing to make this mandate or government takeover of our health care right."
Speaking about President Obama " Call me cynical, but I didn't think his views on marriage could get any gayer."

I was happy to see that Newt Gingrich has staked out a position on the war, a position, or two, or maybe three. I don't know. I think he has more war positions than he's had wives".

"The fundamental reason why Medicare is failing is why the Soviet Union failed, socialism doesn't work. You have ... no price fluctuation".

"I don't like the idea of somebody in Washington deciding that Susie has two mommies is an appropriate family situation and should be taught to my kindergartener at school. That's what happens when we let things get to a federal level".

"Medicare is socialized medicine! People are afraid of that because they'll say "oh, you're against Medicare." No, I'll say "We have to do something different. We can't just eliminate Medicare, but we have to get more to a market-based system."

Senator Paul has threatened to quit and leave politics if the press doesn't leave him alone over his plagiarism. Even his home town paper suggested that he go.

Louie Gohmert (R-TX)
Congressman Gohmert is another pro life, pro personhood wing ding. He said that he "believes that pregnant Muslim women try to visit the US when they are late in their pregnancy so their child can be born here an be a US Citizen with the intent they will raise the child to be a deep

mole type terrorist", he calls them "Terror Babies". Absolutely nuts. He blames the mass shootings like Newtown, on "America's lack of Judeo-Christian beliefs". He believes and supports Michelle Bachman's Muslim infiltrating the government theory.

Actual things that Louie Gohmert has said;

"So when caribou want to go on a date, they invite each other to head over to the pipeline. ... So my real concern now is if oil stops running through the pipeline ... do we need a study to see how adversely the caribou would be affected if that warm oil ever quit flowing?"

"You know what really gets me, as a Christian, is to see the ongoing attacks on Judeo-Christian beliefs, and then some senseless crazy act of terror like this takes place... We've threatened high school graduation participation's, if they use God's name, they're going to be jailed ... I mean that kind of stuff. Where was God? What have we done with God? We don't want him around. I kind of like his protective hand being present."

'I nominate Allen West for Speaker" Gohmert nominated West after he lost his re-election bid.

"This administration has so many Muslim Brotherhood members that have influence that they just are making wrong decisions for America."

"The children could be raised and coddled as future terrorists and twenty, thirty years down the road, they can be sent in to help destroy our way of life."

Eric Cantor (R-VA)
Cantor is the current House Majority Leader. Even though he is actually Jewish, Cantor supports all of the usual right wing pro life anti LGBT issues right along with the Christian extremists. He is firmly against stem cell research. He is pro free trade in any way, shape or form and opposes raising the minimum wage as well.

Actual things that Eric Cantor has said;

"If the Senate fails to pass a measure before April 6, 2011 providing for the appropriations of the departments and agencies of the government for the remainder of fiscal year 2011, H.R. 1 (As passed by The House on Feb. 19, 2011) becomes law." - This was absolutely 100% NOT true.
"Seize the moment, The delay could destabilize the coalition for Obamacare."

"Look, we know we screwed up when we were in the majority. We fell in love with power. We spent way too much money - especially on earmarks. There was too much corruption when we ran this place. We were guilty. And that's why we lost."

Mike Lee (R-UT)
Senator Mike Lee has the highest Conservative rating among the Wacko Bird Crowd with the Club for Growth and the American Conservative Union, rate him as 100% Conservative while The Heritage Foundation gave him a 99% rating.
He falls in line on all of the Tea Party issues. He is buddies with Ted Cruz and stick with him like glue.

Actual things that Mike Lee has said;

"Let's leave Obamacare for another day"

"I'm working, I'll continue to be paid."

Ted Yoho (R-FL)
Ted Yoho is just your run of the mill Tea Party num-num. He stands for all the typical right wing nonsense.

Actual things that Ted Yoho has said;
"I think, personally, it would bring stability to the world markets." Said about the debt ceiling not being raised.

"They said if it is true, it's illegal, he shouldn't be there and we can get rid of everything he's done, and I said I agree with that." Said about president

Obama's birth certificate.

"I talked to a guy that works with Hezbollah, they call him the 007 of Hezbollah, they call him and find out he's brought over 1,500 people here illegally that don't like us, they want to blow us up."

"I had an Indian doctor in our office the other day, very dark skin, with two non-dark skin people, and I asked this to him, I said, 'Have you ever been to a tanning booth?' and he goes, 'No, no need.' So therefore it's a racist tax and I thought I might need to get to a suntanning booth so I can come out and say I've been disenfranchised because I got taxed because of the color of my skin."

Steve King (R-IA)
Pro life, pro guns, anti LGBT, climate change denier, Anti Obamacare, anti immigration, anti affirmative action, pro racial profiling. Nuff Said.

Actual things that Steve King has said;
"I don't want to disparage anyone because of their race, their ethnicity, their name - whatever their religion their father might have been, I'll just say this: When you think about the optics of a Barack Obama potentially getting elected President of the United States. I mean, what does this look like to the rest of the world? What does it look like to the world of Islam? I will tell

you that, if he is elected president, then the radical Islamist's, the al-Qaida, the radical Islamist's and their supporters, will be dancing in the streets in greater numbers than they did on September 11."

"I just haven't heard of that being a circumstance that's been brought to me in any personal way, and I'd be open to discussion about that subject matter." Said about a young woman getting pregnant from being raped.

"The liberals – the environmentalists, the extremists, the Al Gores of the world – were wrong on the science, and today we know it. And I have an Al Gore shower at my place and I took my drill bit out with an eighth-inch bit in it, and I drilled all the holes out so now I can take a shower in three minutes instead of twelve. Sorry Al. But I got a scoop shovel for you if you want to come to any of the fifty states in America. For the first time in the history of keeping records, there is snowfall on the ground in all fifty states. It is tough to make an argument when the evidence is all around us, the snowy white wonder in a crystal cathedral."

"Mr. President, if you're serious about negotiating, then let's do all of the things I've said."

"And at night, the janitors would come through,

which were Nancy's Stasi troops, and screw out those light bulbs, those Edison bulbs, and give me, every once in a while, those curlicue bulbs... So I got this green bag right here. And I filled it up with the black market light bulbs. And I brought them back to my office here in the Capitol. Whenever I need to put a bulb in the lamp, I reach in this green bag and I screw it in there and smile. A little bit of my liberty back. A little bit of our freedom back. And I want to challenge you to do the same thing. Bring back some of that liberty, some of that freedom."

" … they've got calves the size of cantaloupes because they're hauling 75 pounds of marijuana across the desert," regarding illegal immigrants.

Pete Hoekstra (R-MI)
Congressman Hoekstra is a racist and is the guy who ran that anti Asian ad during the Superbowl.

Connie Mack (R-FL)
Another pro life, pro gun, anti LGBT Tea jerk.
Proud Sponsor of the NoBamacare Act

"Let's have a fundraiser and call it legislation!"
Joe Wilson (R-SC)
Another run of the mill Teajhadist with the usual positions

Famous for his one minute of Conservative Tea Party Fame. "You Lie" Yelled at the President on the floor of Congress.

Something Wilson actually said;

"That's offensive to me that they would take my heritage and make it into a Holocaust era type description. I find that very offensive, and it's not true, The Southern heritage, the Confederate heritage is very Honorable."

Then there are the Non elected extremists who use their name recognition and clout to further the extremists agenda, the likes of;

Jim DeMint
Sarah Palin
Joe Walsh
Allen West
Susan Angle
Christine O'Donnell

Nothing they say is of any value whatsoever. They all lost by election, or quit their position. In my view their opinion should hold zero value.

The Koch Brothers

Their father Fred Koch founded Koch Industries, which is the second largest private company in the US. Two of his sons Charles and David control the family business and fortune which they inherited, as well as the Koch Family Foundations. The brothers together are the fourth wealthiest people in the US.

The brothers contribute to many Conservative, Libertarian and Republican Causes and have taken full advantage of the Citizens United SCOTUS ruling literally giving hundreds of millions of dollars, yes, hundreds of millions of dollars across the US to support Republican candidates and their agenda, even down to the local town school board election level.

They are also huge, mongo players in the Oil, Gas, and Chemical lobbying business. They have funded fake studies that show global warming and climate change is a hoax.

Their Father Fred was a founding member of the John Birch Society. The Brothers conservative and religious beliefs stem from him.

These guys are the real deal. No nonsense, put their money where their mouth is, ultra right wing religious, conservative, libertarian, Republican funding juggernauts. Their goal is to build a network of political activists to move the country to the extreme right. They have the will and the funding to do just that. While everyone believed that the Tea Party was a grass roots movement, and it may have been at first, these guys put their money to work hijacking the movement early on to use it for their goals. When the Tea Party rented buses and paid people to demonstrate, they footed the bill. They are willing to put money in almost staggering amounts to work in any election, on any issue that they want to further. While they hire people and use money covertly, they personally like to stay out of the spotlight. They will hide the money in one corporation and move it to another and so on to hide that they are the source. They pay others to get their hands dirty.

The Koch Brothers are the exact reason that the Citizens United ruling must go. There must be transparency and sunlight shined onto this dark pool of money. Their tentacles run so deep they have a nickname, it's "the Kochtopus".

Their main objectives are Repealing the ACA or Obamacare, Denying Climate Change, Fighting Wall Street and Banking Reform, Dismantling Collective Bargaining Rights / Busting the Unions, Eliminating Carbon reductions as well as the EPA, Keeping Corporate Money in Elections,

Fighting Internet Neutrality. Let's not forget the Social conservative issues as well.

Now you can see very clearly, the pattern emerge. All of the Tea Party, Conservatives, and Republicans have the same exact goals, that's because those are the exact goals that the Koch Brothers paid for with their corrupt election funding. Let me put this into perspective for you, these guys spend more money than Exxon, more money than Shell, more money than Conoco, more than BP, more than Chevron. These guys fund the elections, and fund the lobbying. And they damn well expect results. More than the money, they are very well organized, and no doubt, have much more influence than anyone realizes.

Why do they do this? The answer unfortunately is very simple. In order to make their companies far more profitable. Understanding how and why they operate is the first step in countering their efforts to reshape our nation's laws to benefit the wealthy even more than they do today. You have been warned.

They are not the only rich people doing these types of evil things, a fellow by the name of Art Pope has bought 18 Republican wins in North Carolina, a full Republican majority, and got himself appointed Budget Director of the State.

All so his discount stores that are all located in poor ethnic neighborhoods, can keep a steady stream of poor folk buying his merchandise.

These intrusions into our Government and the subsequent law changes that ultimately follow are beyond cruel, beyond racist, beyond Christian, beyond despicable. For shame on them for doing this, and for shame on us for allowing it to happen.

President Obama

President Obama has actually been pretty good for the Country, so far his policies have lowered unemployment to a level before he took office actually adding net jobs. The Markets are at an all time high, corporate profit's are at an all time high, Corporate taxes are at a 60 year low, and 50 million more people now have healthcare coverage. He has reduced by half the overwhelming budget deficit that he inherited. Cut Trillions of dollars from the future deficit. Repealed "Don't ask, Don't tell". Furthered an international diplomacy policy that has reduced the possibility of future armed conflict. Overall one of the best Statesman of our lifetime.

Here are some reactions to anti Obama posts;

There is no Obama TSA Scandal, I looked and Googled and couldn't find a damn thing. Oh wait, are you talking about the illegal searches and seizures authorized by Homeland Security and done by the Bush Administration?
TSA Crapola Debunked.

There is no Obama DHS Scandal. Only the crazy rantings of some wing-nut Republicans like Jim Inhofe who thinks they are buying up all the bullets... Again I would like to remind you that the entire huge giant Government expansion that is

DHS was done by Bush.
DHS Crapola Debunked.

The whole IRS scandal was investigated thoroughly by Darrel Issa and his Conservative Inquisition only to find that there was no Obama connection though they tried and tried. Eventually they figured out that the whole thing was put in motion by a Republican appointee.
IRS Crapola Debunked.

President Obama Supported Egypt's President Morsi because he was the official democratically elected leader of that county. We have a Peace Treaty with them which, to the best of my knowledge, both the US and Egypt kept.

The weapons he gave to Egypt were legal and legitimate under the Israeli-Egyptian Peace Treaty. The weapons that we are going to give to the Syrian Rebels may ultimately wind up in Al-Qaeda's hands, however might I point out that most Republicans including John McCain, Lindsey Graham, etc... want that to happen and actually want even more, hell they want full blown war, or at least that is what they are basically saying. The priest was a Coptic Christian Priest in Egypt, not Syria, and he was shot by supporters of the Muslim Brother hood.

According to thefreedictionary.com The definition of a Treaty; a formal agreement between two or more states in reference to peace, alliance, commerce, or other international relations. in effect a contract. We agreed to and signed that contract. The agreement was that the US would supply 1.3 Billion dollars of military equipment per year. Period. We can not renege on our promise because the situation might have changed. If you sign for a mortgage, you can not simply stop paying the monthly bill because you make less money or your situation has changed. Sequestration has absolutely nothing to do with our International treaties, the sequestration cuts can not be made to treaties. Period.

The United States in NOT going broke, that is just more Right Wing Scare Mongering Propaganda. Let me put that into perspective for you; Do you think that GE is going broke? Do you think buying or owning their stock is an OK thing? they earned profit of $15 Billion dollars on sales of $147 Billion, they have a net profit margin of around 10% Their stock is up 35% over the last year and they throw more than 3% in dividends... are they solvent? Are they in danger of going bankrupt anytime soon? Most reasonable people would say GE is fine, and they would consider buying or owning some of their stock. GE currently has a debt/equity ratio of 3.21 fairly high, but still much lower than many

many other companies including JP Morgan, Pitney Bowes, Clorox, and Lockheed Martin. Do you think any of those companies are about to go bankrupt? Nah, me neither. Now let's compare the Debt/GDP of the US which is approximately 1.3 or 3 times lower than GE and substantially lower that the other companies I mentioned. Therefore the statement that the US is going broke is nonsense. I actually agree with you that we should be spending money on our Veteran's health and benefit's. We certainly could if we wanted to and could get Congress to agree to that. Remember that Congress and not the President holds the purse strings of the country. This is stated very clearly in the US Constitution Article 1, in particular the House of Representatives must originate all spending/appropriations bills. So I am not sure how you are drawing the conclusion that our President is the one cutting corners and/or tossing handouts. This is very clearly in the domain of Congress. If I remember correctly this was covered in 7th grade when we all learned about Government. Here is the strange part, I actually agree with you that we should wean Egypt off of our teat. I would gladly support legislation to renegotiate that treaty. We should renegotiate all of our Foreign aid monies, I would even go so far as to close down many unneeded bases around the world to save money. There is however a correct way to do this and it must originate in Congress. Your anger is misplaced, you should not be angry with President Obama, you should be angry at Congress for not doing their job. If they were on the ball all of those treaties would be under review and negotiation, our veterans would be getting the benefit's that they need. Our Military would be in process of reformation to reduce spending and improve defense readiness in a new century. A perfect example of this is all of those tanks that Congress voted to give the Military even though they don't want them. And for all practical purposes have no use for. Additional nuclear arms funding is another, the F-35 is another. I believe you really need to educate yourself on what is really going on here...

Here is a list of talking points to respond to right wing trolls who post to social media. I have become somewhat of an expert on this. Unfortunately you will find that once your political opponent has lowered him/herself to such a base level that they resort to calling you names and using foul language, it is best to just block them. A wise person once told me "Never argue too long with an idiot, because after a while people will make up their mind as to who the idiot is, however, if you argue too long they wont be able to tell who it is."

Here are the responses to a wrong wing troll.

The first part of each section is what the troll stated, followed by the appropriate response.

America is in a constitutional crisis.

Primarily because we allow people with the educational level of an eighth grader vote, and they always vote Republican, a party that has proven to the nation, time and again, that they couldn't care any less for the poor or the middle class. You, my brainless adversary, are one of those who caused that "constitutional crisis."

Obama is on the verge of impeachment.

Based on what charges? Can you name just one thing the president has done to warrant another tens of billions of wasted taxpayer money on impeachment investigations? And this time around, we're going to demand that, should you try to impeach the president, in return, Bush, Cheney and Rumsfeld all be turned over to the nations who have arrest warrants issued on them, to stand trial for war crimes. The knife will cut both ways, this time.

Obamacare is a death spiral.

Nope. Wrong again, O brainless one! Your own Republican party is in the death spiral. Your side is demanded that the government be shut down unless the ACA was defunded. Your party committed political suicide on a national level, and will be damn lucky if they can field candidates who can win office higher than town janitor outside the former Confederate States.

Obama's outrageous spending is ripping off the people you lefty Libtard's want to help. Or Obama's the one ripping off the poor and middle class

You say that Obama's the one ripping off the poor and middle class? His party is not spending huge amounts of time saying "No" to every jobs bill or infrastructure repair bill put in front of them. It's you people ripping us all off! Perhaps if you pulled your head out of Glenn Beck's backside long enough to see the real world, you'd know that.

Record unemployment is because of Obama's horrible job killing Obamacare.

No, the same obstructionism of Boehner's House on every damn jobs bill, every infrastructure bill, and every bill designed to take care of the people who return home from your wars. By saying "No" to every single thing the president tries to bring to you, is the reason why unemployment, which is not Record unemployment, that was under your boy Bush, isn't going down to pre-Bush levels.

Our national security is compromised.

Remember Robert Rosen of Fox News? Whether or not he was complicit in it, he helped to compromise national security by using Top Secret national security information on North Korea's nuclear program to "scoop the other news networks." The Associated Press was stopped by the NSA from blowing the cover of numerous undercover intelligence agents still in the field. If that hadn't happened, and those gents would've died, you'd be screaming for the president's job even louder than over the bogus scandal of Benghazi. You folks on the right of the aisle would compromise national security if it meant damaging the president's legacy or even help advance your side's wet dream fantasy of a Republican super majority.

The IRS is being used by Obama to crush is political adversaries.

Now, we all know the truth about this. Why you choose to keep up this track is pointless. We all know that both conservative and progressive organizations were targeted by the IRS, and we all know the president had zero involvement and zero knowledge of the BOLO lists. We also know that the Conservative organizations, like True The Vote and the Tea Party groups, all were approved for a tax exempt status they neither were qualified to get, nor deserved to get. And we all know many progressive organizations were denied the same exact status.

The Obama NSA is being unconstitutional by spying on Americans.

How soon we forget the Patriot Act of 2001 was Signed into law by George W Bush, right after the 9/11 terror attack. Obama just re-authorized it. The Patriot act is 100% republican born, and now you're using it against him simply because he's a Democrat?

Obama shut down the pipeline.

The Keystone XL Pipeline was flagged due to environmental concerns (like those of the oil pipeline leak in Arkansas last spring), and aside from that, there are a number of ethical questions Speaker Boehner needs to answer, regarding his stock holdings in numerous companies involved in the pipeline's construction and operation. And then there's the lies about how many jobs the pipeline will create. It's not a couple hundred thousand, as Boehner claims. more like a couple thousand, and maybe a couple thousand more temporary jobs involved in the construction of the pipeline. Finally, there's the ecological disaster being inflicted upon the Alberta province of Canada. There are plenty of photographs showing the damage done by the tar sands oil to the Alberta area. Yet the Canadians are still pushing to get the pipeline built right smack down the middle of America, with no cares about the possible damage a leaking pipeline of the dirtiest oil known to man could do to the water supplies. That oil to be loaded into tankers going to China and East Asia? This is even beginning to do serious political damage to Canadian Prime Minister Stephen Harper and his conservative party.

The scandals... Oh! the scandals... and people died!

The bullshit...Oh the bullshit! There are NO scandals. Your side is batting 0 for 4, and have yet to hit anything other than foul balls in the scandal department. You have nothing on the IRS. Nothing on the AP. Nothing, period! As far as Benghazi is concerned, the only scandal involved there, aside from the fact several Republicans were the ones who edited the talking points, to make it look like the president and former Secretary of State Hillary Clinton doctored them. Is the fact you won't allow Ambassador Stevens and the three men who died with him that night last year, Rest in Peace. You keep exhuming their memories, drag them from their graves and nail them to crosses to score political brownie points with your equally-brain dead base, in the hopes that keeping this up will help you keep your ever growing tenacious hold on your House majority, or your wet dream fantasy of "retaking the Senate." You all over on the right of the aisle should be ashamed of yourselves for using the memories of those four, and your exploitation of their survivors, for political gain. But in order to feel shame, one would have to have a conscience and a soul. And none of you on the right of the aisle have either!

Our schools are crap.

That's something to be laid on the doorstep of the Republican Party. Your side has systematically destroyed our educational system in this nation, and then turned around and claimed that our schools are "liberal indoctrination centers," which you num-num's then use to demand the issuance of "school vouchers," pieces of paper you then use to put your precious NeoCon offspring into either private or religious schools, in the hopes that insulating them from reality will allow you to indoctrinate them to be "Mini me" versions of you and your side of the aisle. And what has your side produced to help our schools? Letting them pray to your prostituted version of Christ and God. Nothing more. Nothing less. Your side of the aisle wrecked our educational system, mainly to produce successive generations of people who will never be able to think critically, or for themselves, relying on a corrupt, corporate media machine to tell them how to do everything short of how to wipe their own butts, and just dumb enough to strengthen their gullibility enough to keep them turning out en masse at the polls to vote Republican without fail.

Is there anything thing of substance the left can point to and say: We made America better?"

There are thousands of things we can point to and say it made things better. Our parents and grandparents left us a world with a system of governmental checks and balances, to ensure we had it just as good as they had it. And then we, the Baby Boomers in charge, took Jim Morrison's famous line, "We want the world, and we want it now!" literally and to extremes, and began systematically dismantling those checks and balances, deregulating everything in sight, allowing corporations to swallow up everything they possibly could, unmindful of the devastation they left behind, and then sit idly by and let the wealthiest one percent of America hoard wealth like a crazy old woman hoards cats, stashing their wealth in safe off shore tax havens in the Cayman Islands, and then amass obscene amounts of profit which they won't share with the people who actually do the hard work in their companies. So they give themselves ginormous bonuses, which go into the same off shore tax havens. Our Fathers made America a country to be proud of. We put you idiots in charge, and you screwed us up.

I say no!

Why not? Your pals Boehner, Cantor and McConnell say that all the time. In closing, all I can say is this, Do us all a favor. Stay home next November. You proved to all of us, above, that you're incapable of separating fantasy from reality.

There is a meme saying how the President is not guaranteeing SS checks blah, blah, blah...

According to the United States Constitution Congress holds the purse strings NOT the President. To be more specific, everything regarding the budget and all Government spending must originate in the House of Representatives. If you don't believe me, by all means, please read it for yourself. If the House does not raise the debt ceiling, all government money will eventually stop. The Treasury department can prioritize who will continue to get paid and who will not. Once the limit has been reached everything stops. All Federal payroll stops. All Government checks stop. All government agencies close. The United States will have it's credit rating sliced and down graded and when the House finally decides to let the Government run again everything will cost more. Treasury notes, bills, and bonds interest will immediately triple if not more. Every company worldwide that has a contract will immediately sue the Government for damages and breach of contract. It would be fairly catastrophic. The Government was actually shut down twice back in 1995 by then Speaker Newt Gingrich and his Republican thugs. Mr. Gingrich became the first Speaker of the House in our history to be thrown out and censured by Congress. Look it up, it's all on the internet. It just amazes me that ignorant people are trying to blame the President. Maybe, just maybe if you had paid attention in 7th grade when they taught US Government or again in 9th or 10th grade you would understand how this all works. So if you actually believe that President Obama is to blame and is the reason that military payrolls stop or grandmas SS check stops, you are the dupe. Why don't you write, email, or call your Republican Congressman and tell him that you understand how our Government works and if he votes to shut down the Government you will vote him out. This blather about the president is pure Right Wing Propaganda, all the while the Conservatives and the Republicans are holding us all hostage to their ideology. And you fell for it. Now how smart do you feel?

Obamacare

A friend wrote:

Incentives matter. People pay attention to them. The larger the incentive, the more effective it is. Look at Obamacare. You get heavy subsidies right up to exactly 400% of the poverty line. Then you get nothing, you go directly from being heavily subsidized to being the subsidy, all for that extra dollar in income. This might easily mean for a married couple that they pay an extra $10,000 a year for the same health insurance policy (more or less depending on specifics, but this number is not atypical). Then look at the fact that a lot of employers are shifting to providing employee-only health insurance, and dropping coverage for spouses and dependents.

If a working couple are each making $30k a year, they receive a significant subsidy. If one gets a promotion that comes with a 10% raise ($3,000), then it kicks them into zero subsidy land, and the net loss of $7,000 a year. The incentive for divorce in order to make ends meet is powerful, because if they divorce, then they both qualify for a bunch of other programs, too, which would effectively boost their effective incomes considerably. Meeting bills vs not meeting bills, being able to afford vacation vs not... This ACA thing is a powerful incentive that, if it stands more than two years, will drive a HUGE boom in

divorce and application for "single parents with kids needing government assistance."
Obamacare is the most destructive bill to American society I've ever witnessed pass congress.

I took a look at the actual numbers using the exact criteria laid out in the letter.

In a nutshell if your combined income is less than $90k per year your family will get about $45 per $1000 in subsidy. Zero above $90k

If we take the example your friend used combined income of $60k the actual cost under ACA would be $4913 per year or 8.19% of their income, that seems reasonable doesn't it? If one of them got a raise of $3000 they would then pay $5,392 or 8.56% of their income. the difference would be $479

Conservatives have basically said something similar about Social Security, which has actually been the most effective poverty tool in US history. They fought tooth and nail against Medicare and Medicaid as well. None of these things have had any detrimental effect to the American Family or structure.

Actually these programs have helped families because now Grandma and Grandpa can live with a roof over their head instead of living in the street or being a financial burden to their kids. What your friend failed to take into account is that that same family paying for private insurance, even if it's thru their job would, on average, be much more anyway. So her whole argument is bunk.

The average healthcare premium before Obamacare is about $800 per month per family or $9600... after the raise they would be paying $5,392 under Obamacare and thus saving well over $4000

Funny what happens when you look at actual facts instead of Right Wing Propaganda talking points.

You can verify all of the premium and subsidy info here:
http://kff.org/interactive/subsidy-calculator/

Syria

The Assad military detained some rebels that were supposedly Al Qaeda associated so they then paraded them in front of TV cameras to try and convince the US that they are really the good guys. In response to that ploy, the Rebels are trying to claim that Assad had used Sarin gas to prove somehow that they are the good guys. The reality of all this is that there is no definite proof that Assad himself ordered any kind of chemical weapons attacks of any kind anywhere. All of the so called proof is "suspect" with no actual "Chain of custody". Therefore No "Red Line" has been crossed.

Even if it turns out that some Commander somewhere actually did order a gas attack, this is not what the President was talking about. The "Red Line" would be an actual attack like what was done to the Kurds in Iraq. That attack in Halabja killed between 3,200 and 5,000 people, and injured around 7,000 to 10,000 more. Nothing like that has occurred in Syria. Period.

Now here is the more alarming fact, most of the Rebels fighting the Assad Regime are Islamic Extremists. None or very few of the Rebels are secular or what you might call Moderate or Liberal Muslims. Most if not all are Jihad extremists that want nothing short of an Islamic state if they win.

Now that you understand what is actually happening there. What do you think we should do? The Neo Conservative Republicans in Washington such as John McCain, Lindsey Graham, Saxby Chambliss, and Mike Rogers are beating the war drums and are demanding a "call to arms". They make the argument that if we show any "sign" of weakness that will somehow cause us to lose a war with Iran? The pretzel logic here astounds me. They demand that we start arming the Rebels. So let me get this crap straight, they actually want us to give guns and ammo to Al Qaeda and other Islamic Extremists? Of interest here is that these are the same blithering idiots that made us do that in Afghanistan with Osama Bin Laden and the Mujahideen. They also swore in every way imaginable that there were WMD's in Iraq. We saw this before and it sucked.

The bottom line is there is no way in hell we should get involved militarily in Syria, this is nothing short of an absolute quagmire waiting to happen. Another war would completely destroy us, we can not afford it, there is no reason to fight it, and who do you think would pay for it? Above all think of the thousands of US Soldiers that would die, and tens of thousand injured.

The Truth about Syria is we don't know if the Syrian Government used banned gas on it's people. We don't know if the rebels did it to their own and are now pointing a finger at Assad. We may never know for sure.

Frankly why do we even care? Both the Rebels and the Government are basically both sworn enemies of the United States. The Government is Muslim and has supported terrorism against the US , Israel, the EU and other places around the world. The Assad regime has supported terrorist groups like Hezbollah and Hamas for decades. The rebels fly the black flags of Al Qaeda. All of the rebels are Islamic extremists of one type or another, none at this point are secular.

The NeoCon's are beating the war drums again for Syrian intervention and for profit's of the US Militarily Industrial Complex. Lindsey Graham and John McCain never came across a war they didn't like. The likes of these idiots would have us spend another couple of trillion dollars just so they can get their kickbacks.

The US absolutely needs to stay out of Syria, no matter what. To hell with the so called "Red" lines. The bottom line on this is there is no freaking way in hell we should get involved militarily in Syria, this is nothing short of an absolute quagmire waiting to happen. Another war would completely destroy our economy, we just can not afford it, there is no good reason to fight it, and just who do you think would actually pay for it? Above all else think about the thousands of poor US Soldiers that would die, and tens of thousand more that would surely be injured.

Let the Countries around Syria lead first. Turkey has already said they pretty much want no part of it. Then let Europe decide, or the Arab League, then NATO and the UN. If any or all of those people can put together a coalition, then maybe we can help them out some.

We are not the World Police and should not interfere with the affairs of other Nations. Have we learned nothing from Iraq, Afghanistan, or Vietnam? Wage Diplomacy and Peace for a while and see how that fairs.

Labor

Major Reasons Why You Should Thank Unions.
Benefit's hard fought and won by unions in this
Country.

Weekends
All Breaks at Work, including your Lunch Breaks
Paid Vacation
FMLA
Sick Leave
Social Security
Minimum Wage
Civil Rights Act/Title VII (Prohibit's Employer
Discrimination)
8-Hour Work Day
Overtime Pay
Child Labor Laws
Occupational Safety & Health Act (OSHA)
40 Hour Work Week
Worker's Compensation (Worker's Comp)
Unemployment Insurance
Pensions
Workplace Safety Standards and Regulations
Employer Health Care Insurance
Collective Bargaining Rights for Employees
Wrongful Termination Laws
Age Discrimination in Employment Act of 1967
Whistleblower Protection Laws
Employee Polygraph Protect Act (Prohibit's
Employer from using a lie detector test on an

employee)
Veteran's Employment and Training Services (VETS)
Compensation increases and Evaluations (Raises)
Sexual Harassment Laws
Americans With Disabilities Act (ADA)
Holiday Pay
Employer Dental, Life, and Vision Insurance
Privacy Rights
Pregnancy and Parental Leave
Military Leave
The Right to Strike
Public Education for Children
Equal Pay Acts of 1963 & 2011 (Requires employers pay men and women equally for the same amount of work)
Laws Ending Sweatshops in the United States

A True Progressive Agenda

Political Reform
Citizens United v FEC Overturned by
Amendment and Elimination of Money as free
speech
Political Campaign Contributions Reformed
reasonable limit's imposed and Fully Transparent
Lobbying Reformed, Restricted and Fully
Transparent
Eliminate all PAC and Super PAC's, also
eliminate all tax exempt groups like the 501c
except for 100% humanitarian and public health
and safety groups
All Corporate and special interest money made
illegal though elimination of corporate and
religious money

Term Limit's
All Elected Officials provided Medicare or pay out
of pocket for their healthcare
Any Elected Official convicted of any Felony
Immediately is ousted from public office and
forfeit's all of their pension and or any other
Government service entitled.
Politically purchased advertisements must pay
fair market price
Political ads,candidates, representatives and
elected officials as well as party members
subject to libel and scandal laws
All State Distracting Maps to be reviewed and

adjusted on a regular basis by non partisan
private committees or the Department of Justice
Civil Rights and Liberties
Patriot Act repealed
Voter ID laws Unconstitutional as a Poll Tax
Marriage Equality
Equal Rights for Gay and Transgendered citizens
All Civil Liberties Re-Instated
Abolition of "Right to Work" States
Medicare for All
Better Free Public Schools and Education
including College
Forbearance of All School Loans

Woman's Rights
Full Reproductive Rights for Women
Equal Rights Amendment Ratified
Abortion on demand in all public hospitals

Immigration
Immigration Free and Legal
Full Amnesty for all non convicted Felons
Citizenship allowed for any and all provided they
are not convicted Felons

Commerce
All Government Corporate Subsidies stopped
Big Banks broken up and Re-Instate the Glass–
Steagall Act
A Financial Transaction Tax
Stronger Pollution Controls

More Alternate Energy
The Internet Free and Neutral
Higher Taxes on the Wealthy
Churches and Religious Groups Taxed
Tax cuts for any corporations creating jobs or investing in alternate energy, manufacturing, business start ups, and small business

Economy
Raise the minimum wage and tie future raises to an index, perhaps CPI

Industry
Energy policy defined, moving away from fossil fuels and toward renewables
Safety rules enacted for hydraulic fracturing (Fracking) and added back in to the Clean Air and Clean Water Acts

Military
All Wars & Foreign Entanglements Ended
Nuclear Weapons Reduced and Secured
Guantanamo Bay Closed
End Policy of Policing the World and close Military Bases where unneeded
Military Budget Reduced
Cancel F-35 Contract

Government Inefficiencies
Dissolve the Dept. of Homeland Security and divide responsibilities between the Coast Guard, National Guard, Secret Service, The NSA and The FBI
A US Infrastructure Policy Defined and Funded
A US Energy Policy Defined and Passed
All US Natural Resources companies to pay a portion of their profit's to fund Social Security, Medicare, Medicaid, Education, and Welfare
All Federal Employees provided Medicare or pay out of pocket for private insurance

Health Care
100% Socialized health care for all US citizens

Free Society

If we are a free nation and we believe in rugged individualism and capitalism, why then are there businesses that we are not allowed to engage in or run?

Millions of jobs would be created and additional tax revenue would easily be in the hundreds of billions.

Hemp
Hemp is a sustainable resource that can be used to create thousands of different products including fuel, fabrics, paper, household products, and food and has been used for hundreds of centuries by civilizations around the world.

Marijuana, Cocaine, Opium, Heroin, and all other drugs
Ending the "War on Drugs" would save tens of billions in tax dollars. Legalization of drugs would facilitate the freeing up of resources used to police, prosecute and incarcerate offenders. Would create jobs and dramatically increase tax revenue.

Prostitution
Save money on prosecutions and incarcerations. Create jobs and tax revenue. Create better public

health and help prevent the spread of sexually transmitted disease or STD's.

Gambling
The strongest argument for legalizing gambling is also the simplest, individual liberty. A free society where the government bans activities it finds immoral or unseemly is not really a free society.

Assisted Suicide
Patient autonomy. A patient should have the right to control the circumstances of his or her own death and to determine how much suffering is too much.

Mercy. If a patient's pain and suffering cannot be relieved with current medical care, then the doctor has an obligation to do everything within his or her power to help that suffering, even to the point of speeding up the death process if there are no real alternatives for the patient.

Non abandonment. A doctor has an obligation to their patient, as well as to the patient's family to be there for the dying process and to be as responsive as realistically possible.

Fireworks
We can buy 50 caliber anti aircraft guns without any checks but a bottle rocket is out of bounds? There is no reason an adult should not be

allowed to buy basic fireworks. The high powered stuff that the Grucci Family uses maybe would have some restrictions, but even then training and permit's should be sufficient.

24/7 Alcohol

We are allowed to buy chocolate 24 hours a day, 7 days a week, 365 days a year. If something is legal it's legal, if not then it's not. Blue laws that not allow the purchase or consumption of any legal product is just ridiculous.

Absinthe

Just like other alcohol doesn't effect everyone the same way. Legalizing absinthe is just like the argument to legalize marijuana, something as harmful or more harmful is legal why isn't this?

Gay Marriage

In a truly free society we should be allowed to marry whomever we chose, period.

Polygamy

If all parties are in favor, why not? Nobody is harmed and if one understands natural science you can extrapolate that there are many more women in the world than men, if polygamy was legal then everyone's chances to not be alone would improve. That's not to say polygamy would be defined as more than one wife, rather as a marriage of more than 2 people.

Abortion on demand
Women should have 100% complete reproductive freedom, period. Not your belly, not your business.

Contraception
All contraception should be legal and available to all men and women of any age, period.

It's all really very simple either we are a truly free society and a free Country, or we are not. Either we are all free to choose what we do and consume or we are not. Do we live in a Free State or a Nanny State? A Regime of Liberty, or a Totalitarian Regime? A Nation of individualists or a Fascist Nation? A people controlled by the people or the Religious Zealots? Or are we a Nation of individuals who can decide their own lives for themselves?

Liberal Accomplishments

Here is a list of Major Liberal Accomplishments that have been enacted into law and have bettered America and / or American citizens economically.

1. The 40 hour work week
2. Weekends, Saturday and Sunday off
3. Vacations and/or Vacation time
4. Woman's Voting Rights
5. The Civil Rights Act of 1964
6. The right of people of all colors to use schools and facilities.
7. Public schools.
8. Child-labor laws
9. The right to unionize
10. Health care benefit's
11. National Parks
12. National Forests
13. Interstate Highway System
14. GI Bill
15. Labor Laws and Worker's Rights
16. Marshall Plan
17. FDA to make sure our food and pharmaceuticals are safe
18. Direct election of Senators by the people, previously they were picked by each States legislature
19. OSHA Occupational Safety and Health Administration, Workplace safety laws

20. Social Security
21. NASA
22. The Office of Congressional Ethics. Created in 2008.
23. The Internet
24. National Weather Service
25. Product Labeling and Truth in Advertising Laws
26. Rural Electrification and the Tennessee Valley Authority
27. Morrill Land Grant Act
28. Public Universities
29. FDIC Bank Deposit Insurance and SIPC Securities Investor Protection Corporation
30. DC Centers for Disease Control and Prevention
31. Consumer Product Safety Commission
32. Public Broadcasting and Educational Television
33. ADA Americans With Disabilities Act
34. FMLA Family and Medical Leave Act
35. EPA Environmental Protection Agency
36. Clean Air Act
37. Clean Water Act
38. USDA the US Department of Agriculture
39. Public Libraries
40. Transcontinental Railroad and the rail system in general
41. Civilian Conservation Corps
42. Panama Canal
43. Hoover Dam

44. The Federal Reserve
45. Medicare
46. The United States Military
47. FBI
48. CIA
49. Local and state police departments
50. Fire Departments
51. Veterans Medical Care
52. Food Stamps
53. Federal Housing Administration
54. Extending Voting Rights to 18 year olds
55. Freedom of Speech
56. Freedom of Religion and the Separation of Church and State
57. Right to Due Process
58. Freedom of The Press
59. Right to Organize and Protest
60. Pell Grants and other financial aid to students
61. Federal Aviation Administration and Airline safety regulations
62. The 13th Amendment outlawing slavery and involuntary servitude
63. The 14th Amendment giving citizenship to freed slaves and due process for all Americans
64. The 15th Amendment affirming all citizens right to vote
65. Unemployment benefit's
66. Woman's Health Services
67. Smithsonian Institute
68. Head Start
69. Americorps

70. Mine Safety And Health Administration (This has been weakened by conservatives, resulting in recent mining disasters.)
71. Food Labeling
72. WIC
73. Peace Corps
74. United Nations
75. World Health Organization
76. Nuclear Treaties
77. Lincoln Tunnel
78. Sulfur emissions cap and trade to eliminate acid rain
79. Earned Income Tax Credit
80. The banning of lead in consumer products
81. National Institute of Health
82. Garbage pickup/clean streets
83. Banning of CFCs.
84. Erie Canal
85. Medicaid
86. TARP
87. Bail Out of the American Auto Industry
88. Lily Ledbetter Fair Pay Act
89. Wildlife Protection
90. End of Don't Ask Don't Tell
91. Established the basis for Universal Human Rights by writing the Declaration of Independence
92. Miranda Rights
93. Banning of torture
94. The right to a proper defense in court
95. An independent judiciary

96. The right to vote
97. Fair, open, and honest elections
98. The right to bear arms (Do you really think extreme right wingers would allow anybody besides themselves to have firearms if in power?)
99. Health care for children and pregnant women
100. A stable and strong government established by a Constitution
101. The founding of The United States of America
102. The defeat of the Nazis and victory in World War II
103. Paramedics
104. The Brady Handgun Act
105. The Glass-Steagall Act (It has since been repealed and we've been paying the price for it.)
106. Oil industry regulations (The Gulf paid the price after conservatives tore many of these regulations down.)
107. The Affordable Care Act which makes insurance companies more honest and fair.
108. Woman's Right to Choose
109. Title IX
110. Affirmative Action
111. A National Currency
112. National Science Foundation
113. Weights and measures standards
114. Vehicle Safety Standards
115. NATO
116. The income tax and power to tax in general,

which have been used to pay for much of this list.
117. 911 Emergency system
118. Tsunami, hurricane, tornado, and earthquake warning systems
119. Public Transportation
120. The Freedom of Information Act
121. Emancipation Proclamation, which ended slavery
122. Antitrust legislation which prevents corporate monopolies (These laws have been savaged by conservatives, which is why corporations are getting huger and competition is disappearing leading to less jobs and high prices.)
123. Water Treatment Centers and sewage systems
124. The Meat Inspection Act
125. The Pure Food And Drug Act
126. The Bretton Woods system
127. International Monetary Fund
128. SEC, which regulates Wall Street. (Conservatives have weakened this regulatory body, resulting in the current recession.)
129. National Endowment for the Arts
130. Campaign finance laws (Conservatives have gutted these laws, leading to corporate takeovers of elections.)
131. Federal Crop Insurance
132. United States Housing Authority
133. Soil Conservation
134. School Lunch Act

135. Mental Retardation Facilities and Community Mental Health Centers Construction Act

136. Vaccination Assistance Act

137. Over the course of nearly 50 years, liberals contributed greatly to the eventual end of the Cold War.

138. The creation of counterinsurgency forces such as the Navy Seals and Green Berets.

139. Voting Rights Act, which ended poll taxes, literacy tests, and other voter qualification tests.

140. Civil Rights Act of 1968

141. Job Corps

142. Elementary and Secondary Education Act of 1965

143. Teacher Corps

144. National Endowment for the Humanities

145. Endangered Species Preservation Act of 1966

146. National Trails System Act of 1968

147. U.S. Postal Service

148. Title X

149. Kept the Union together through Civil War and rebuilt the South afterward.

150. Modern Civilization

Not to mention the repeal of prohibition and legal alcohol, so every time you have a beer, a drink, or a glass of wine, you better thank a Liberal.

Conclusion

I had a dream.

I dreamt that the American people finally understood, and they voted out all of the Tea Party Congressmen. All of the Neo-Con's gone. Right Wing-nuts removed. McConnel, Canter, Boehner, Cruz, Ryan, Bachman, and a slew more all gone. Sanity returned and we had a Democratic majority in the House and Senate. Bills began to pass, laws signed, a true sea change occurred.

The Minimum wage was raised and tied to inflation. The Wait staff loophole removed. Full time and part time defined, temporary worker limitations enacted.

"Right To Work" was abolished, Unions and Guilds one again could collectively bargain for better working pay, safety, and mobility. Taft-Hartley reformed to encourage organizing.

Legislation passed to reverse the out sourcing of Jobs passed, giving tax breaks to companies that create US jobs and penalize companies that offshore jobs.

A.L.E.C. Members defect and the organization goes belly up. The Heritage Foundation Fails and closes it's doors. The Tea Party Express loses a wheel and crashes in a ravine. Journalism is revived and laws passed that make News "Not for Profit' and all reporting must be the truth. The FCC pulls FOX's license and they go off the air. All Media conglomerates broken up, syndicates cracked. Complete unconsolidation of all media from corporate control. Rush Limbagh is criminally indited, Glen Beck falls off the wagon and is discredited, Bill O'Reily is fired, Sean Hannity ostracized, and Ann Coulter is caught in bed with Megan Kelly. The Tea Party is added to the Terrorist watch list as a "hate group". It was my Liberal dream after all. LOL

Financial regulation became very strict, the too big to fail money center banks were broken up. Dodd-Frank was made bulletproof, Glass-Steagall was re-approved into law. Levered ETFs were made illegal, the up-tick rule came back. Dark pools were eliminated. Offshore profit's had to be repatriated or full taxes were to be paid on them. Derivatives were paired down to basics. Leverage on all exchanges and banks reduced.

Tax reform was passed away from the income tax and to the "Fair Tax" a consumption tax on everything except basic foods and clothing. The IRS was shut down, never to be seen again.

The Social Security Tax or FICA maximum limit

was gone, so that now everyone pays an equal fair share percentage.

An Energy policy was finalized which included Solar, Wind, Geothermal, Hydroelectric, Hydrogen, Ethanol, Wave & Tidal. This policy stated America is to be 100% Fossil Fuel Free within 50 years. Renewable energy only after that. Safety rules were put in place or strengthened on Oil & Gas drilling both onshore and off, Deep water drilling was stopped. Tar Sands Oil banned, pipelines firmly regulated. All spills and blowouts to be cleaned 100% at the expense of the company found liable. Period. Exxon was forced to clean up Prince William Sound, BP the Gulf., etc... Hydraulic Fracturing safety rules were defined. Mining Operations safety was addressed. EPA Emissions were finally fully limited for all type fossil fuels. MPG requirements for cars, trucks, boats, trains, and aircraft all went way up. The Clean Air and Water Act was improved and strengthened. We joined the Kyoto Protocol. All oil subsidies go away. We adopted the "Nordic Model" and all company profit's on oil, gas, coal, uranium, and all other natural resources were taxed additionally and the profit's used to fund Social Security, Medicaid, and Medicare.

We adopted the French and German Health care models and true Socialized Medicine became the law of the land for every man, woman, and child. All citizens would have 100% coverage for life, for health, hospitalization, prescription, eye care, and dental, etc... Abortion "On Demand" available to every woman at every public hospital in the Country. Contraception available over the counter to everyone as well.

We adopted the Australian model of "Pay It Forward", education and higher education was available for everyone. The Finnish and South Korean models for public education were adopted and funded.

All GMOs were made illegal. Bee killing pesticides were abolished. Protocols were put in place to grow Switch grass for ethanol production, Hemp was made legal, Marijuana was made legal. Farm subsidies were limited to Family farms and Organic farms. Antibiotics and Hormones banned. Pink Slime eliminated for consumption.

Legislation passed to stop "excessive" packaging of for sale products, recyclables became the reality, no more Styrofoam cups and plates, no more plastic blister packs, no more shrink wrap. Paper and cardboard only. Mandatory recycling in every community nationwide.

Gun controls were put in place, background

checks, 100% registrations, Mental evaluations, licenses and insurance mandatory. Assault Rifles banned just like machine guns, high capacity magazines outlawed. All Federalized so that all States are on board and oversight by the ATF.

The Military budget was cut in half. No more "Big Boy" toys until the deficit is brought under control. The practice of Military Privatization completely reversed and stopped. Diplomacy became the National doctrine. No more drone strikes. The Department of Homeland Security and the NSA completely disbanded, defunded, and shut down. Same with the FISA Court. The 'Patriot Act" repealed, "Warrant less" wiretaps revoked. "Extreme Rendition" abolished, "Stop loss" stopped, Due process and all individuals Rights restored. Enhanced interrogation eradicated. Two thirds of all military bases around the world shuttered and given back to their home countries. No more Empire building. The war in Afghanistan ended, All of our troops completely out of the Middle East.

The VA fully funded and fixed. Completely integrated so as soon as one of our veterans is separated from active duty their VA plan kicks in. This includes re-entering civilian life counseling, Stress and Trauma PTSD counseling, fully automatic benefit's. No more paperwork and wait nonsense.

All Federal, State, and local privatization completely stopped and reversed. Including all prisons. Prison reform so that anyone previously convicted for small quantities of drugs have their sentences commuted and they are released. After a felons time is served their voting rights are reinstated. Racial injustices is addressed within the Justice system. Racial profiling becomes a recognized crime and the DOJ enforces the law. The "War on Drugs" stopped immediately and the focus moved toward rehabilitation and education started.

Article 4 of the "Voting Rights Act of 1965" is replaced with "All States" and the DOJ can review and stop any State law or restrict any change in any State law regarding voting laws. Federal mandates for all States on extending Early Voting, removal of all Voter ID laws, assessment and restriction of redistricting or "Gerrymandering". Any States found to be engaged in the "Southern Strategy" or employing "Jim Crow" laws shall have all their Federal funding halted until such time as they regain compliance. Severe penalties for infractions. Social Justice Equality for all, blacks, minorities, women, LGBT, etc...

A Constitutional Amendment fully repealing "Citizens United v FEC" stating that "Corporations are NOT people", and "Money is

NOT Free Speech". Campaign reform enacted to remove all money from Politics. PACs and Super PACs are gone. Term limit's imposed on all public offices. The Filibuster returned to it's original construct, bills passed or failed on a straight up or down majority vote. Budgets held to account and adjusted to keep in accord with GDP. Elimination of debts and deficit's through automatic taxes and cuts thereby removing the "Politics" from the accounting.

Immigration reform passed that opened up our borders to anyone seeking a better life for themselves and their families, the only restrictions would be if they have a communicable disease or are a convicted dangerous Felon. Just like it used to be for the first two hundred years of our history. All would be encouraged to seek citizenship. The Dream Act passed allowing a pathway to citizenship for all of those trapped outside or within the current system.

A return to complete "Separation of Church and State", "Under God" removed from the Pledge just as it originally was. All mention of God taken off of our Currency. All churches and religions made to pay taxes just like everyone else. The US Motto changed from "In God we Trust" back to the much more reasonable " E Pluribus Unum".

Besides the Legalization of Marijuana, all other drugs as well as Prostitution, Gambling, Assisted Suicide, Absinthe, Marriage Equality, Polygamy, Legalized, Regulated, and Taxed. All available 24/7 so as to promote actual freedom, and increase tax revenue. A True Free State.

Welfare and Food Stamps funded and expanded so that that anyone who needs help can get immediate relief and longer term mentoring with education, occupational training, rehabilitation and treatment. A whole person/whole family approach to actually address and fix problems rather than enable failure.

A National Infrastructure Bank was established and funded, all of our bridges, tunnels, roads, ports, railroads, parks, electric grid began to be upgraded, repaired, replaced, or expanded. A Public works program started so that any able bodied person who wanted a job could sign up and start immediately.

Full implementation of a true "Trickle Up" Economy, where all of the citizens of this great Nation can once again participate and believe in the American dream.

As I drank in all of these changes, everyone who wanted a job was now working. Earning an actual living, not just a wage. Keeping more of their real wages because of the new tax reforms. Our economy growing strong and steady, our knowledge and wealth increasing. All elderly, sick, and disabled now taken care of. Our children are safer. Our technology going forward and our Mother Earth breathing a sigh of relief... it was at that moment that I woke up and realized what "could be" versus "what is", and I began to cry... realizing that I will likely never see this in my lifetime, my America, my dream of America is lost. The American dream is gone. Period. We are on the cliffs edge, the Fascists are in control and the people are on the losing side. Only you getting involved and voting can bring a return to sanity.

I can only hope that you agree with at least some of what I have said here and are angry now too.